AMERICAN SCHOOLS OF ORIENTAL RESEARCH
PALESTINE ARCHAEOLOGICAL MUSEUM

DISCOVERIES IN THE JUDAEAN DESERT
OF JORDAN · IV

THE PSALMS SCROLL OF QUMRÂN CAVE 11

(*11QPs[a]*)

BY

J. A. SANDERS

OXFORD
AT THE CLARENDON PRESS
1965

Oxford University Press, Amen House, London E.C.4

GLASGOW NEW YORK TORONTO MELBOURNE WELLINGTON
BOMBAY CALCUTTA MADRAS KARACHI LAHORE DACCA
CAPE TOWN SALISBURY NAIROBI IBADAN ACCRA
KUALA LUMPUR HONG KONG

PRINTED IN GREAT BRITAIN
AT THE UNIVERSITY PRESS, OXFORD
BY VIVIAN RIDLER
PRINTER TO THE UNIVERSITY

FOREWORD

THE American Schools of Oriental Research take pleasure in making available this volume of the publication of the Dead Sea Scrolls.

This Psalms Scroll was edited by Professor J. A. Sanders, of the Colgate Rochester Divinity School, a task undertaken while under appointment of the American Schools as Annual Professor in Jerusalem in 1961–2.

This scroll was among those of Cave 11, Qumrân, purchased from the Bedouin some years ago by the Palestine Archaeological Museum in an effort to save them from destruction. Since then the ownership has been transferred to the Government of the Hashemite Kingdom of Jordan in accordance with the recently adopted view that the scrolls were one of the country's most important natural assets.

With the approval of the Council of Ministers of the Kingdom of Jordan, the museum was given permission to sell to appropriate academic institutions both the copyright and the right to publish the various scrolls.

In the autumn of 1961 the American Schools of Oriental Research purchased the publications right and the copyright of the Psalms Scroll with funds which were made available through the generosity of Kenneth K. Bechtel and Elizabeth H. Bechtel. We are especially indebted to the latter for her deep and abiding interest in the affairs of the Schools, particularly in connexion with the Dead Sea Scrolls.

We are also most grateful to Frank Moore Cross, Jr., of Harvard University, who, as chairman of the Schools' Special Committee on the Dead Sea Scrolls, and also as a member of the International Committee on the Scrolls, has had administrative direction of this and other recent projects of the Schools relating to the scrolls, to Père Roland de Vaux, the general editor of the series, and to Yusef Saʿad, Curator of the Palestine Archaeological Museum, for their assistance in making this publication possible.

A. HENRY DETWEILER
President
American Schools of Oriental Research

PREFACE

THE scroll was unrolled in November 1961.[1] This manuscript leaves the editor's hands in December 1962.

Preparation of the scroll for publication, in such a comparatively short period of time, would have been impossible without the assistance of a score of mentors, colleagues, students, and friends.

My mentor in America is Professor Frank Moore Cross, Jr., of Harvard University. Were it not for him I would not be the editor of this volume; and were it not for him the oversights and errors contained herein, for which I am solely responsible, would be many more. My mentor in Jerusalem is Père Roland de Vaux, O.P., chief of the international team of Dead Sea Scroll scholars and President of the Board of Trustees of the Palestine Archaeological Museum; his encouragement and wisdom guided me through the winter of recovery in the museum and in the library of the École biblique et archéologique, of which he is director.

Dean A. Henry Detweiler, President of the American Schools of Oriental Research, and Dr. Paul W. Lapp, director of the Jerusalem School of the ASOR, have skilfully administered all external affairs relating to the scroll. As Annual Professor in the Jerusalem School during 1961–2 I was given every consideration and encouragement to fulfil the task assigned me by the ASOR, which hold the copyright of the scroll.

At the museum the Curator, Mr. Yusef Saʿad, made available the facilities necessary for unrolling and studying the scroll. Mr. Saʿad's long experience in Dead Sea Scroll affairs is a comfort to those whom he graciously encourages and helps. His resources include those of his staff, whose services are invaluable: Mr. Najib Albina, the photographer of the museum, whose work is the best in his field, and Mr. Hamdi Nubani, the secretary of the museum and a linguist of note.

The library of the École biblique in Jerusalem is a model for libraries in biblical studies, and the Dominican scholars who work there are generous savants in their fields. Père J.-P. Audet gave freely of his time and wisdom, especially in the area of hellenistic thought, and Père F.-M. Lemoine in Syriac studies. A student there, Père Louis Khalifé, professor in the Scolasticat du Saint Esprit in Kaslik-Jounieh, Lebanon, also gave valuable assistance with the Nestorian texts.

During a visit to Jerusalem, Professor David Noel Freedman convinced me that the first line of Col. xxvii contains the last six words of II Sam 23^{7}, despite the misleading variant which appears there. And Monsignor Patrick W. Skehan, who, with Father Louis Hartman, translated Ecclesiasticus for the Confraternity Bible (1955), convincingly identified xxi 11 ff. as Sirach $51^{13\text{ ff.}}$, despite the wide differences in the texts. I am also indebted to Professor Skehan for permitting me to study the 4Q psalms fragments which he is assigned to edit and for his many valuable suggestions generally.

Professor John Strugnell, of Duke University, has scrupulously checked all the notes in the critical apparatus in Part II and, indeed, throughout the volume. He has generously given of himself to the cause of accuracy and preciseness: whatever errors and inexactitudes remain are my responsibility alone.

The Colgate Rochester Divinity School through its President, Gene E. Bartlett, has shown

(1) Cf. *Bulletin of the American Schools of Oriental Research*, clxv (1962), pp. 11–15.

a rare understanding of what had to be done by permitting me a year's sabbatical followed by a semester of semi-seclusion in which to do it. To three of our students, David Lutz and John Wiberg, who assumed the burden of preparing clean, neat copies of the transcriptions and critical apparatus, and Stephen Peterson, who double-checked the index, I am pleased to say, 'Well done'.

It is by the generosity of Elizabeth Hay Bechtel and Kenneth K. Bechtel that the scroll is made available to scholarship, and the editor is pleased to dedicate his work on it to them.

J. A. S.

Rochester, New York
15 December 1962

Postscriptum. It has been a distinct pleasure to work on the proofs and revises as they have come from the Clarendon Press. The gentlemen of the Press have been exceedingly patient in permitting numerous author's alterations and additions in proof, and while I wish that it were possible to include in this volume all the various readings available to date of Ps 151 (cf. *infra* p. 54, n. 4), or to account by theory for every point of orthographic interest in the scroll (cf. *infra* p. 14, n. 1), such extensive addenda are manifestly impracticable at this late stage.

Search for truth is rooted in a fear of falsehood, and no man alone can find the one, or shun the other. Scholars will note, as I continue to see, further needs for improvement: and that is, as it should be, reason sufficient to go to press without further delay.

J. A. S.

30 October 1964

CONTENTS

TABLE OF PLATES xi

I. INTRODUCTION

A. DATA, CONTENTS, AND INDEX 3

B. PALAEOGRAPHY 6

C. ORTHOGRAPHY 9

D. SURFACE OBSERVATIONS 13

II. TEXT

TRANSCRIPTION AND APPARATUS 17

SIGLA, ABBREVIATIONS AND SIGNS 18

III. THE APOCRYPHAL COMPOSITIONS

Nos. I, II, and III of the Five Syriac Apocryphal Psalms		53
Ps 151 A, B—(Syriac) Ps I	Col. XXVIII, ll. 3–14	54
(Syriac) Ps II	Col. XVIII	64
(Syriac) Ps III	Col. XXIV, ll. 3–17	70
Plea for Deliverance	Col. XIX	76
Sirach $51^{13\text{ ff.}}$	Col. XXI, ll. 11–17, Col. XXII, l. 1	79
Apostrophe to Zion	Col. XXII, ll. 1–15	85
Hymn to the Creator	Col. XXVI, ll. 9–15	89
David's Compositions	Col. XXVII, ll. 2–11	91

INDEX OF HEBREW WORDS IN THE APOCRYPHALS 94

TABLE OF PLATES

(at end)

I. *a*. The scroll before unrolling, 10 November 1961
b. The scroll partially unrolled, 16 November 1961

II. Unrolling completed, 20 November 1961. 11QPs[a] Col. XXIII

III. Fragments A, B, C, and D of 11QPs[a]

IV–XVII. Columns I–XXVIII of 11QPs[a]

I
Introduction

A

DATA

11QPs[a], the Psalms Scroll from Qumrân Cave 11, was found by Arab Bedouin and brought to the attention of the officials of the Palestine Archaeological Museum in Jerusalem, Jordan, in early February 1956. Other documents and scores of fragments from the same cave were also purchased by the Museum.[(1)] Among the fragments only four have been identified as belonging to the Psalms Scroll; they are written in the same hand and on the same type of material as the scroll itself. The scroll was unrolled in the Museum between 10 and 20 November 1961.[(2)]

The scroll is tanned animal skin, deep yellow to brown in hue, considerably darker than the infra-red photographs would indicate. It lacks little of being 1 mm. thick. It is exceptional in this regard, and P. W. Skehan has suggested it may be calf skin rather than the accustomed goat skin of Qumrân.

The four fragments, which contain parts of Pss 101, 102, and 109, probably derive from the sheet or sheets immediately preceding the extant sections of the scroll. The four fragments are here assigned the letters A to D (right to left on pl. III). Frags. A and B and the partial column on the right of frag. C form what survives of one column of the text of Pss 101^{1}–102^{2}. The greater part of frag. C, the left column, contains parts of Pss 102^{18}–103 (?$104)^{1}$. Frag. D contains the ends of lines forming a part of Ps 109^{21-31}. These three columns of text are indicated as follows: frags. A, B, C I, frag. C II, and frag. D.

Four separable leaves form the first columns of the scroll proper. Decomposition along one side of the rolled scroll had destroyed the three or so layers of leather which had originally been continuous. The fourth leaf connects at one line of text with the scroll at the point where it becomes continuous. From that point the scroll measures 3·89 m. in length.

The top margin of the scroll is everywhere evident, even in the fragments. A feature of the scroll's appearance, which cannot be detected in the photographs, is the arc which it forms when rolled out fully, sheet to sheet. The top of the scroll, at the upper margin, is clean, supple, and well preserved. The bottom of the scroll, by contrast, is in an advanced state of decomposition, black and brittle, causing drawing and shrinkage (see Surface Observations). The disintegration of the threads connecting the sheets began always at the bottom, due to the tension created by the lack of a surface large and long enough to permit the scroll to lie on the arc it would have described. The tendency of the scroll to 'draw' in this manner is apparent in pl. VIII to the left of col. xiii, where the threads were, at the moment of photography, still intact and every attempt was being made so to handle the material that the threads would be preserved. Soon after the photograph was taken the fine threads disintegrated, leaving no traces. The threads at the top of the connexion, which are visibly of coarser texture than the original and represent reparation sewing in antiquity, are (to my knowledge) still in place.

At their widest points, length and width, the fragments (pl. III) measure: frag. A, 7·2 × 3·7 cm.; frag. B, 4·7 × 4·2 cm.; frag. C, 13·1 × 9·4 cm.; frag. D, 11 × 5·1 cm.

(1) Cf. *Revue biblique*, lxiii (1956), pp. 573–4.

(2) Cf. *Bulletin of the American Schools of Oriental Research*, clxv (1962), pp. 11–15. Among the Cave 11 fragments assigned to Professor J. van der Ploeg and to be published by the Royal Dutch Academy are several of both canonical and non-canonical psalms. It is for this reason that the siglum for our scroll has been changed from 11QPss, as it appears in *BASOR* clxv, to 11QPs[a].

The four separable leaves (cols. i–v, and part of vi—pls. IV–VI) measure, at their widest points, 9·8 cm., 11 cm., 12 cm., and 14 cm. respectively in width of column, and 16 to 17 cm. each in length of column, or width of scroll including top margin.

The five sheets (left part of col. vi to the end—pls. VI–XVII) measure, at their longest points, at the top margin, 25 cm., 81 cm., 87 cm., 72 cm., and 77 cm. respectively in length, and from 15 to 17·9 cm. in width.

Line spacing varies from 0·85 to 1 cm. Margins at the top vary from 1·8 to 2·1 cm. and the ruled margins between the columns vary from 1·7 to 3 cm. The average column margin is 2 cm., but it expands to as much as 3 cm. where sheets connect. Indentation, at the beginnings of compositions, varies from 1 to 4·5 cm. where it occurs (see Surface Observations).

The following table (omitting the fragments) gives measurements in centimetres, by columns, at the widest line of writing and at the longest span, including top margin.

Plate	*Column*	*Line width*	*Column length*
IV	i	3 cm.	17 cm.
	ii	6	17
	iii	11	16·5
V	iv	12	16
	v	9	16·2
VI	vi	13·5	16·2
	vii	11·7	16·4
VII	viii	13	16
	ix	11·5	16·3
VIII	x	10·6	16·7
	xi	13·3	17
IX	xii	10·2	17
	xiii	9·9	17·5
X	xiv	13·3	17·4
	xv	13·5	17·3
XI	xvi	13·2	17
	xvii	13·6	17·2
XII	xviii	12	17·5
	xix	12	17·5
XII	xx	12·7	17·9
	xxi	13	17·8
XIV	xxii	12·7	17·6
	xxiii	12·3	17·5
XV	xxiv	11·3	17·5
	xxv	12·7	15·6
XVI	xxvi	12·8	15·3
	xxvii	12·8	15
XVII	xxviii	13·9	15

Caution should be exercised in using the photographs to note measurements; while generally speaking of natural size, they fall somewhat short of full measure.

Edge to edge, disregarding lacunae, there is a total of 4·112 m. of leather remaining of the original scroll. While it is impossible to estimate accurately the original length of the scroll, the original width can be determined with some certainty. Since Ps 119 is copied in the scroll in the alphabetic acrostic arrangement of eight verse-lines to the letter, the width can safely be adjudged to have been 25 to 26 cm., approximately that of $1QIs^{a}$.

CONTENTS

Frags. A, B, C I	Ps 101^{1-8}
	102^{1-2}
Frag. C II	102^{18-29}
	103 (?104)^{1}
Frag. D	109^{21-31}
Col. i	105^{25-45}
ii	$146^{9-?-10}$
	148^{1-12}
iii	121^{1-8}
	122^{1-9}
	123^{1-2}
iv	124^{7-8}
	125^{1-5}
	126^{1-6}
	127^{1}
v	128^{4-6}
	129^{1-8}
	130^{1-8}
	131^{1}
vi	132^{8-18}
	119^{1-6}
vii	119^{15-28}
viii	119^{37-49}
ix	119^{59-73}
x	119^{82-96}
xi	119^{105-20}
xii	119^{128-42}
xiii	119^{150-64}
xiv	119^{171-6}
	135^{1-9}
xv	135^{17-21}
Col. xv	Ps 136^{1-16}
xvi	$136^{26b(?)}$
	$118^{1, 15, 16, 8, 9, ?, 29(?)}$
	145^{1-7}
xvii	$145^{13-21+?}$
xviii	(Syriac) Ps II
xix	Plea for Deliverance
xx	Ps 139^{8-24}
	137^{1}
xxi	137^{9}
	138^{1-8}
	Sirach $51^{13\ ff.}$
xxii	51^{30}
	Apostrophe to Zion
	Ps 93^{1-3}
xxiii	141^{5-10}
	133^{1-3}
	144^{1-7}
xxiv	144^{15}
	(Syriac) Ps III
xxv	Ps 142^{4-8}
	143^{1-8}
xxvi	149^{7-9}
	150^{1-6}
	Hymn to the Creator
xxvii	II Sam 23^{7}
	David's Compositions
	Ps 140^{1-5}
xxviii	134^{1-3}
	151 A, B

INDEX

II Sam 23^{7b}	xxvii 1
Ps 93^{1-3}	xxii 16–17
101^{1-8}	Frags. A, B, C I 1–10
102^{1-2}	Frags. A, B, C I 11–12
Ps 102^{18-29}	Frag. C II 1–11
103 (?104)^{1}	Frag. C II 12
105^{25-45}	i 1–16
109^{21-31}	Frag. D 1–9
$118^{1, 15, 16, 8, 9, 29(?)}$	xvi 1–6
119^{1-6}	vi 11–16

Ps 119^{15-28}	vii 1–14	Ps $136^{26b(?)}$	xvi 1
119^{37-49}	viii 1–13	137^{1}	xx 17
119^{59-72}	ix 1–14	137^{9}	xxi 1
119^{82-96}	x 1–15	138^{1-8}	xxi 1–10
119^{105-20}	xi 1–16	139^{8-24}	xx 1–16
119^{128-42}	xii 1–15	140^{1-5}	xxvii 12–15
119^{150-64}	xiii 1–16	141^{5-10}	xxiii 1–6
119^{171-6}	xiv 1–6	142^{4-8}	xxv 1–5
121^{1-8}	iii 1–6	143^{1-8}	xxv 6–15
122^{1-9}	iii 7–14	144^{1-7}	xxiii 12–17
123^{1-2}	iii 15–16	144^{15}	xxiv 1–2
124^{7-8}	iv 1–2	145^{1-7}	xvi 7–16
125^{1-5}	iv 3–8	145^{13-21}	xvii 1–17
126^{1-6}	iv 9–15	146^{9-10}	ii 1–5
127^{1}	iv 16	148^{1-12}	ii 6–16
128^{4-6}	v 1–3	149^{7-9}	xxvi 1–3
129^{1-8}	v 4–9	150^{1-6}	xxvi 4–8
130^{1-8}	v 10–16	151 A, B	xxviii 3–14
131^{1}	v 17	(Syriac) Ps II	xviii
132^{8-18}	vi 1–10	(Syriac) Ps III	xxiv 3–17
133^{1-3}	xxiii 7–11	Sirach $51^{13\ ff.}$	xxi 11–17 xxii 1
134^{1-3}	xxviii 1–2	Plea for Deliverance	xix
135^{1-7}	xiv 7–15	Apostrophe to Zion	xxii 1–15
135^{17-21}	xv 1–5	Hymn to the Creator	xxvi 9–15
136^{1-16}	xv 6–17	David's Compositions	xxvii 2–11

Note also Pss 33^{8} and (?)145^{10-12} in ii 1–4; Jer 10^{12-13} (51^{15-16}) and Ps 135^{7} in xxvi 13–15; and Ps 143^{2b} in xxiv 7.

B

PALAEOGRAPHY

No tracing of the letters is offered. The scribe's hand in the infra-red photographs is so clear that the following observations may be made directly on the accompanying plates. Caution should be exercised against using only one column of text for palaeographic study and especially against taking the initial letters of lines in Ps 119 as norm.

The first palaeographic observation which must be made is that wherever the TETRAGRAMMATON appears in the scroll it is written in the Palaeo-Hebrew script. It may be omitted where MT has it (e.g. iii 6); it may be replaced by אדוני (e.g. vi 1) or by אלוהים (e.g. xxiii 14); or it may appear in the scroll where no other witness has it (xvi 7 and xxi 2, both with scribal dots). But wherever it occurs it is in the ancient script.

The following observations are made directly on the basis of Frank M. Cross's master-paper, 'The Development of the Jewish Scripts', *The Bible and the Ancient Near East*, the W. F. Albright *Festschrift*, edited by G. Ernest Wright, 1961, with particular emphasis on fig. 2

(pp. 138–9) and the accompanying discussion (pp. 166–81). His own earlier work, as well as that of W. F. Albright, E. L. Sukenik, Solomon Birnbaum, N. Avigad, and others, receives full treatment in the paper. Furthermore, it includes judicious judgements based on Professor Cross's study of unpublished materials. It is the definitive work to date on early Jewish scripts and there need be no apology for basing present observations principally on his evaluations of such a vast wealth of material.

With due consideration given to possibly individual characteristics the script of 11QPs[a] is clearly comparable to lines 5, 6, and 7 of Cross's fig. 2. It exhibits the heavily drawn, large script most popular in the late Herodian era; however, a number of letter forms have not yet evolved fully into the late style.

The *'alef* combines the major characteristics of the later Herodian period: the inverted V configuration of the left and right legs, and the *keraia* at the top of the right arm. The right arm sometimes joins the right leg, sometimes not.

The *bet* has lost the tick on the right shoulder of Hasmonaean character. The lack of the right shoulder tick is sometimes the only clear distinction between *kaf* and *bet*. The right shoulder is sometimes square, sometimes distinctly rounded. The base stroke appears to be made from right to left, although in some instances it extends beyond the vertical right downstroke. The scribe's pen turns from the downstroke into the base and out to the left. The *bet* is a good example of a transitional script of the middle Herodian period.

The right leg of the *gimel* has a distinct thickening at the top in many instances, and often appears to be quite straight or only slightly bent. The left leg extends from about midway of the right and curves downward in most instances. This parallels the description of the *gimel* in 4QDan[b]. Other examples of the *gimel* give the distinct impression of an inverted Y.

It is difficult to determine whether the *dalet* was made in a continuous stroke of the scribe's pen or not. There are extremely few instances of which one could unequivocally say that the horizontal bar breaks through the vertical leg. In the great majority of the cases one could as well say that the downstroke is continuous with the horizontal by the scribe's having turned his pen at the right shoulder in the change of direction from right stroke to downstroke. The result is a distinct *keraia* on the right shoulder which is the principal distinction between the *dalet* and the *resh*. The *dalet*, too, seems to indicate a transitional script of the middle Herodian period.

The crossbar of the *he* is heavily shaded, with the left end heavily triangular. One would say that *he* was made by a continuous pen stroke starting with the lower right leg, in the manner described of 4QSam[a]. There is no distinct projection of the horizontal bar to the right. In fact, the only real distinction between *ḥet* and *he* is the triangular projection of the crossbar to the left. The *he* exhibits traits characteristic of the late Hasmonaean period.

Waw and *yod* are distinguished in the scribe's mind, not always by his pen, and not in ligatured forms. The shaded, angularly hooked head of *yod* tends to be broader, the leg shorter (except in ligatured forms, of course), and the stance slightly less vertical than those of *waw*. They seem to be similar to *yod* and *waw* in 4QDan[b].

The *zayin* is a simple stroke thickened at the top. The 'thickness' has more of an orientation to the right than to the left; the head is not bent.

The crossbar of the *ḥet* is not as heavily shaded as that of the *he*, nor does the left shoulder project out as far as that of the *he*. Because the crossbar was made with the thinness of the scribe's pen rather than its thickness, the crossbar appears often to dip, forming a bowl with the two angular shoulders, which remain similar in appearance.

The *ṭet* appears to be made in two movements, from the left arm into the base, and then the curled right head and downstroke. It gives a broad, squat appearance and the tip of the left arm is distinctly thickened to the right.

The medial *kaf* is long but not narrow, and certainly not squat. The top is little more than a sharp downward curve from left tip to right. The right leg is straight and the base departs from it cleanly without loop, angle, or *keraia*. The base of the *kaf*, however, slants downward slightly, rather than straight across as is typical of the *bet*.

The final *kaf* is hardly different from the *dalet* save in the length of the downstroke (see the word וידידיך in xxii 8), which is rigidly straight in most examples, curving only slightly in others. It has some affinities with Cross's fig. 2, l. 8, P. W. Skehan's 4QPss material, and is seemingly late Herodian.

The hook of the *lamed* is distinct, but the tail forms less of an angle with the horizontal interval than might be expected. In some few cases it is drawn almost on a parallel with the long upper arm, straight down. The top of the arm is thickly shaded into a triangle in some cases, but characteristically has a left *keraia*, again similar to Skehan's 4QPss hand.

The medial *mem* seems to have been made in two strokes. The left oblique probably was made last, drawn right to left, in 'Early Herodian Style', though the form is developing in the direction of late Herodian *mem*.

The final *mem* is consistently closed. The left vertical stroke crosses the top horizontal bar but is straight. The letter gives the impression of being long but not slender. The top bar is relatively long, protruding well to the left with a distinct *keraia*. The right downstroke leaves the bar cleanly at an angle, and is straight, in most examples, until it curves into the left vertical stroke. It has affinities with the final *mem* of the late Hasmonaean period, and is an instance of the survival of this older type into the Herodian period, as is sometimes the case with final *mem*.

At the top of the downstroke of *nun* is a thickening or bend oriented to the right; frequently it is triangular, but is rarely a real *keraia*. It seems closest to the *nun* of 1QM.

The final *nun* is essentially an S-shaped curve, often thicker in the middle of the stroke than at the top, which only rarely can be said to exhibit even a rudimentary *keraia*.

The most distinctive feature, perhaps, of the *samekh* is its almost rigidly flat leg and crossbar. It appears to have been made with an initial upstroke forming the left leg, a loop into the crossbar, and an arc to complete the enclosure. The *samekh* only rarely forms a triangle. It is most similar to 4QDan[b].

The right arm and left leg or tail of the *ʿayin* are one stroke. The right arm is essentially a vertical *keraia* out of which the leg breaks sharply to the left and rigidly straight without curving. The left arm was penned separately, most often neatly joining the tail, a few times failing quite to join, and a very few times breaking through the tail. The left arm has a *keraia* to the left. Not infrequently the tail of the *ʿayin* ligatures with a following *waw*, the result being a fairly good *shin* with misplaced middle horn. The *ʿayin* has affinities with some examples of the *ʿayin* in 1QM, but is larger, with a developed thickness at the top of the left arm.

The head of *pe*, medial and final, has a tendency to curl in toward the right downstroke, though this is not consistent. There is no evidence of a tendency to angle in. The closest analogy again seems to be the *pe* in 4QDan[b].

The right arm of the *ṣade* is for the most part a triangular *keraia*. The left arm thickens to the right in many cases, but to the left in others, especially in final *ṣade*. The tail of medial *ṣade* breaks sharply to the left in all instances, at or only slightly below the 'base line'. The tail of final *ṣade*, like that of final *kaf*, plunges deeply below the line.

Qof was made with one pen stroke vertically up, looping into the crossbar, with a sharp break down and back to the left. The crossbar is rigidly flat; and the final arc fails, in the great majority of cases, to touch the leg. The leg only irregularly can be said to start below the base line. It has characteristics in common with 1QM and with 4QDeut[j].

The left shoulder of the *resh* is consistently a full pen point, turning sharply, sometimes at an acute angle, into the horizontal bar. The right shoulder is often an angle, but also quite often rounded. The distinction between *dalet* and *resh* is in the right shoulder; the former has a tick, the latter has not.

The right lower leg of *shin* is drawn like that of *'ayin*, sharply bent. The right arm is little more than a vertical full pen point breaking sharply into the right leg, leaving the arm looking like a *keraia*. The middle horn is a very thin, simple stroke which frequently fails to join the left leg, in the manner familiar in 1QH (first hand) and 4QDan[b].

The *taw* was made in one continuous stroke from left leg to right, the top of the left leg being a simple loop into the right. *Taw* has broadened from early Herodian styles, and is quite like those of 4QDan[b] and 4QDeut[j].

Most traits of the hand of 11QPs[a] are characteristic of hands transitional from early to late Herodian, though a few letters exhibit early characteristics (*he*, final *mem*), and some late (*kaf*, *'ayin*). The hand has most traits in common with the developed Herodian hand of 4QDan[b], but possibly is slightly earlier. A date in the first half of the first century A.D. may be assigned.

C
ORTHOGRAPHY

WAW AND *YOD*

THE scribe distinguished between *waw* and *yod*, except in those cases where ligatured forms tend to obliterate even the slight distinction. Of 135 instances where *waw* and *yod* occur side by side without an intervening letter: 109 times the *yod* is shorter; 17 times they are of the same length; and 9 times the *yod* is longer than the *waw*. Hence, in approximately 80 per cent. of such combinations the scribe made a distinction. On the distinguishing traits other than length, see above the paragraph on *waw* in the section on palaeography.

These observations are made on the basis of the readings in MT in the case of the biblical psalms, and on the basis of the most probable readings in the case of the apocryphal compositions.

PLENE AND DEFECTIVE READINGS

The *waw*

Generally speaking *ḥolem*, *shureq*, *qibbuṣ*, and *qameṣ ḥaṭuf* are indicated by *waw*. For example, among nouns which occur frequently, כול, עולם, מואדה (MT מאד), רואש, and קודש are consistently written with the *waw*. The adverb לוא, as well, is consistently written with a *waw*.

Ḥolem defectivum in nouns and adjectives is apparently indicated in the following instances:

מצֹות xi 11
עֹשק xii 7
גבורֹתיכה xvi 12
נפשֹתֶכמה xviii 1
אלֹה xx 11
עֹצב xx 16
עֹז xxi 5
גבֹה xxi 7
בתֹרה xxi 11
חלֹמות xxii 14
מכמֹריו xxiii 6
חטאֹתי xxiv 7
חטאֹת xxiv 11
יֹם xxvii 8
הגבֹהים xxviii 9

Nouns with a *qibbuṣ* are written with *waw* except תֻשבחתך in xxii 11. Among pronouns only the suffix of ידורשוהֻ in vi 12 lacks the *waw*.

Nouns with a *qameṣ ḥaṭuf* are always written with a *waw* with one exception: גלמי in xx 7.

The qal imperfect verb has *ḥolem plene* (e.g. יפולו xxiii 6) with the following exceptions only:

תעמֹד x 9
תחמֹל xviii 14
ותֹאחזני xx 2
יֹאמרוך xx 12
(cf. יואמר v 4)

The qal imperative verb has the *waw* in all instances except ברֹק in xxiii 16. However, the imperative with suffix occurs three times with *waw* and twice without it:

סמכני xi 12
חקרני xx 14
שמורני xxiii 5
זכורני xxiv 10
שומרני [*sic*] xxvii 15

Similarly, the qal infinitive has the *waw* except שרֹף in xxvii 1.

The qal active participle regularly has the *waw* with the following apparent exceptions:

חלומים iv 10
בֹטח xv 2
עֹשה xvi 2
יֹדעת xx 6
פֹלח xxiii 3
בֹקע xxiii 3
יֹרד xxiii 9

The puʿal verb regularly has a *waw* (e.g. רוקמתי xx 7) with the following apparent exceptions:

עֻשיתי xx 6
יֻצרו xx 8
ותהֻמם xxiii 17

The single instance of a *waw* omitted in the plural verb ending is תתבעֻך in xxii 14 (if that is the correct reading).

Whereas the *waw* is included in יכולו (v 5) and even in יקושו (xxiii 5) it is omitted in יגֹרתי (viii 3). Cf. יגרו in xxvii 14.

It should be carefully noted that the above listings are the apparent exceptions. The scroll, generally speaking, exhibits *plene* spellings (cf. note *infra* p. 14).

Qameṣ ḥaṭuf

The *qameṣ ḥaṭuf* of MT is indicated by a *waw* with the exceptions noted above: סמכני xi 12, גלמי xx 7, and חקרני xx 14 (?).

The following list is exhaustive with the exception of (1) the חיני–חונני problem which is dealt with below, and (2) the occurrences of כול. כול is always spelled so whether in the construct state or not; it is not included in the list.

בתום־לבבי	Frags. A, B, C I 2	בזוכרי	xix 12
ישמור־צאתכה	iii 6	קודשכה	xxi 3
וחוצנו	v 8	אוזני	xxi 14
אוזנכה	v 11	קודשכה	xxiv 4
חוקכה	ix 6	אוזנכה	xxiv 4
עוזרני	x 5	פועלכה	xxv 11
וחונני	xii 5	קודשו	xxvi 3
עוניי	xiii 4	בקודשו	xxvi 4
לעוזרני	xiv 3	בחוכמתו	xxvi 14
אוכלמה	xvii 6	ולקורבן	xxvii 7 *bis*
קודשו	xvii 16	החודשים	xxvii 8
חוכמה	xviii 3	למושחני	xxviii 8
אוכלמה	xviii 11		

What the pronunciation of these words was in the Herodian period is another question: suffice it here to emphasize that with the noted exceptions, wherever, according to Massoretic 'grammar' we should expect the *qameṣ ḥaṭuf*, a *waw* appears.

Under this heading there is a special problem. Compare the following MT and 11QPs[a] readings:

MT	*Q*		*MT*	*Q*	
חיני	חונני	viii 1	חיני	[*sic*] חיני	xiii 5
חיני	חונני	viii 4	חיני	חונני	xiii 7
חיני	חונני	x 7	חיני	חונני	xiii 11
חיני	חונני	xi 3	Apoc.	[*sic*] חונני	xix 14
חנני [*sic*]	חונני	xii 5			

The case of xiii 5 indicates that the scribe could see (hear?) חיני; the list cannot indicate an individual peculiarity of the scribe. The case of xii 5 but confirms the other readings. Contextually חונני is a possible reading in each case where it stands. We should and must assume that the scribe reliably transmitted what he received. N.B.: חונני occurs as well in 4Q *Catena*[a] ii 3 assigned to J. M. Allegro.

There are a number of interesting occurrences of the *waw* which should be noted.

It was pointed out above that the various forms of the qal imperfect verb regularly have the *ḥolem plene* with the second root-letter (e.g. ואשמורה in x 7). In the scroll there are five cases, however, where *waw* occurs after the first root-letter:

ישומרכה	iii 5	אדורשנה	xxi 12
ידורשוה	vi 12	[*sic*] ותחושבהו	xxiii 15
יעוזרני	xiv 5		

The following should be noted as exhibiting uncommon occurrences of *waw*:

בארמונותיך	iii 12	עודי	vi 5
עוזרנו	iv 1	פותאים	xii 3 xviii 3, 4
עקלקולות	iv 7	חנום	xiii 13
חלומים	iv 10		

The *yod*

The appearance of *yod* in the scroll is generally consistent with Massoretic orthography, but exhibiting *plene* readings. דויד always appears with the *yod* (agreeing with the spelling in Chronicles, e.g., as against MT Psalms) as well as ירושלים.

There are two nouns which lack the expected *yod*:

אלומותו iv 15	נפשתֿכמה xviii 1

The expected *yod* is omitted in six verbs:

והעבֿר	xv 15
יחשֿך (MT יחשיך)	xx 3
נעֿמו (N.B. *yod* erased)	xxiii 3
הוצא (MT הוציאה)	xxv 4
יכתֿרו (N.B. *yod* erased)	xxv 5
ויוצא (cf. ויוציא in xv 13)	xxvi 14

Note the following uncommon occurrences of *yod*: לשונינו (erased and corrected to לשוננו) in iv 10, שבותינו in iv 13, זידים (cf. זדים in vii 7 ix 11 and xviii 13) in x 4, and מיתי in xxv 10.

The *'alef*

The appearance of *'alef* in the scroll is generally consistent with Massoretic orthography; e.g., כי never has the *'alef*. The exceptions are:

ולו (? cf. MT ולא—see apparatus *ad loc.*)	xx 8
בתרה (for בתוארה)	xxi 11
מודי (cf. מואדה)	xxii 1
לצונו (cf. הצואן in xxviii 6, 11)	xxviii 4
התור (for התואר)	xxviii 9

Only תובד, in xxii 8, among verbs lacks the expected *'alef*.

The following words exhibit an unexpected *'alef*:

אזרוע (MT זרוע)	xv 14
נפלאות (? MT נפליתי)	xx 5 (see below)
אשאול (MT שאול)	xxiii 4

The *he*

With one possible exception, the 2nd masc. sing. perf. verb has the תה— ending (e.g. גערתה in vii 7). In xx 5 the reading may be נפלאית (with LXX[BA] Vulg PR Syr), but if so, it is the single instance in the scroll where *he* is lacking in such a verb; hence, the probable reading is נפלאות with the resultant contextual problems.

Similarly, the 2nd masc. sing. suffix has the כה— ending (e.g. ידיכה in frag. C II 8) with only six exceptions: תורתך in xii 15, רעיך in xx 9, יאמרוך and עריך in xx 12, יודוך in xxi 5, and פיכ in xxi 6, where the *he* has been erased but the medial *kaf* left standing. The כה— ending is found where MT has a pausal form, e.g. עמכה (MT עמך) in xx 10. The *he* may have been omitted in אתה in vi 14.

By contrast the 2nd fem. sing. suffix always has the final *kaf* without *yod* (see iii 8–14 and xxii).

There is a preference exhibited in the scroll for the *he* ending or cohortative form of the 1st sing. impf. verb without suffix; 36 times it occurs with *he* and 18 times without.

Twice the *he* is omitted where it is expected: אלוהיכמ in v 9, and הרב in v 15, and once erased but still visible, in xxi 6.

הואה occurs once, in xviii 6. The 2nd masc. pl. suffix has the *he* once, נפשתכמה in xviii 1.

The 3rd masc. pl. suffix has the *he* in the following words (cf. המה in xi 7):

במה	x 12	אמריהמה	xviii 12
אוכלמה	xvii 6	להמה	xix 3
להמה	xvii 6	מהםה	xix 6
שועתמה	xvii 12	מהמה	xx 9
אוכלםה	xviii 11	ברעותיהמה	xxiii 2
שתותמה	xviii 11	נכבדיהםה	xxvi 2

MISCELLANEA

In addition to the above observations there are a few words to which attention should be called but which fall outside the above categories:

עמנו		iv 12	טמוט	(MT תמוט)	xxii 17
מבטוב	(MT מבטוח)	xvi 4	ותלפתי	(MT ותפלתי)	xxiii 1
לבטוב	(MT לבטוח)	xvi 5	אבעים	(for ארבעים)	xxvii 9
באח	(MT אחד)	xx 8			

D

SURFACE OBSERVATIONS

SCRIBAL DOTS

SCRIBAL dots (cf. *Num. Rabbah* 3, *Aboth deRabbi Nathan* 34; M. H. Segal, *Journal of Biblical Literature*, lxxii (1953), p. 42) occur in four places in the scroll. This observation is based on the scroll leather itself; caution should be exercised against mistaking worm holes for dots and vice versa. In two instances the dots are placed both above and below the letters, in both cases the TETRAGRAMMATON in the Palaeo-Hebrew script: xvi 7 and xxi 2. In the other two instances the dots are placed over the letters only: xiv 5 and xxvii 1 (erased).

INSERTIONS

There is only one possible marginal marking in the scroll, an extraneous configuration in the lower extremity of the margin to the left of col. xxii.

Letters or words were inserted, in the hand of the original scribe, above lines of text, twenty-four times.

iii 2	xvi 10 *bis*, 15	xxiv 12, 13
vii 13	xvii 6 *bis*	xxv 9, 11, 12
viii 6	xix 8	xxvii 2
xii 13	xx 9, 17	xxviii 3, 11
xiii 5, 6	xxiii 6, 12	

ERASURES

There is clear evidence, in twenty-eight *loci*, of erasures in the text. There is no reason to think that any was made by another than the scribe himself. He but very rarely wrote over an erasure (iv 10 xxvii 1).

i 15	xviii 9	xxiii 3, 14
iii 8, 11	xix 2, 4	xxv 5 *bis*, 9, 12
iv 10, 14	xx 1, 3, 13	xxvi 12, 13
vi 2	xxi 5, 6	xxvii 1
xi 7	xxii 10 *bis*	xxviii 7
xv 11		

Extreme caution is urged against locating further evidence of erasure on the basis of the photographs, in which worm traces and scar tissues in the skin may be misleading.

SPACING

There are fourteen *loci* in the text where the scribe avoided writing on the leather either because of poor tanning preparation or because of scar tissue in the skin. Some of the areas are quite small and some quite large (e.g. col. xviii).

viii 3	xx 3, 8 *bis*	xxvi 6, 13
xiv 8	xxii 7–8	xxvii 2–4
xv 2–3, 8–9	xxiii 8	xxviii 10
xviii 6 ff.		

Spaces are left blank at *loci* other than those listed in the above two categories. Entire lines are skipped between the strophes and at the end of Ps 119 (but not at the beginning; cols. vii–xiv), between Pss 118 and 145 (col. xvi), and between Pss 134 and 151 A (col. xxviii). All compositions, in fact, are separated by spacing: either by indentation (cols. iii iv v xvi xxiii xxv xxvi xxvii), or by leaving some portion of a line unwritten, with the possible exception of xvi 1 (see apparatus). Such spacing is easily recognized for its purpose.

There are a few spacings in the scroll, however, which do not fall under any of the above categories, the explanations for which should be otherwise construed (iii 4 viii 6 xii 12, &c.).

SHRINKAGE

There is one further necessary caution which should be exercised in using the photographs. As in many another ancient manuscript, there are instances of leather shrinkage in the scroll which could lead to unwitting errors in estimating lacunae. Sometimes shrinkage gives the appearance of a gap larger than that which actually exists. Such cases are to be found near and at the bottoms of cols. xiv xv xviii xxii and xxiv (see apparatus).

The accompanying critical apparatus and notes are intended, in part, to aid in avoiding errors which might arise due to such phenomena as are listed in the several foregoing paragraphs.[1]

[1] The above orthographic observations are based on MT traditions and should not be construed as indicating the earlier vocalization to the exclusion of other possibilities (cf. *infra* apparatus and notes).

II

Text

TRANSCRIPTION AND APPARATUS

ONLY those lines in the scroll which contain writing, or would have contained writing, are numbered in the transcription: all lines are numbered except those which are completely devoid of writing (in cols. vii–xiv, xvi, and xxviii, already listed above, in Part I, under 'Spacing').

The apparatus contains reading notes to the text of the biblical psalms. The few necessary reading notes to the eight apocryphal compositions are contained in the critical notes accompanying the translations below, in Part III.

The variants noted in the apparatus are those readings in 11QPs[a] which differ from MT—except that the consistent orthographic differences which are listed above under 'Orthography' are not noted in the apparatus. The apparatus indicates support in the early witnesses for the variants.

The following list of sigla and bibliography indicates what has (and what has not) been included in the apparatus: only those critical editions of ancient texts which appear in the list have been consulted; the apparatus does not pretend to operate beyond them.

SIGLA

1Q11:1	*DJD* i, p. 71 (Ps 126[6])
4QPs[h]	Fragments of psalms from Qumrân Cave 4, assigned to P. W. Skehan
Q	11QPs[a], the Psalms Scroll (used in this edition only)
MT	*Biblia Hebraica*[3], R. Kittel, Ed. ktb ketib, consonantal text qere' vocalized text
Ken	*Vetus Testamentum Hebraicum cum Variis Lectionibus*, B. Kennicott, Ed., 1780
de Rossi	*Variae Lectiones Veteris Testamenti*, J. B. de Rossi, 1784–8
Grk	The Greek witnesses, as follows:
LXX	*Psalmi cum Odis* (*Septuaginta*, vol. x), A. Rahlfs, Ed., 1931 *The Old Testament in Greek*, vol. ii, H. B. Swete, Ed., 1891
Hex	*Origenis Hexaplorum Quae Supersunt &c.*, Tomus ii, F. Field, Ed., 1875 *'Εβρ* Greek Transliteration — *Θ* Theodotion *Α* Aquila — *E'* Quinta *Σ* Symmachus — *ς'* Sexta *O'* LXX — *Z* Septima
Lat	The Latin witnesses, as follows:
Vulg	*Biblia Sacra Iuxta Latinam Vulgatam Versionem ad Codicum Fidem*, vol. x: *Liber Psalmorum ex Recensione Sancti Hieronymi*, 1953
PR	*Le Psautier romain et les autres anciens psautiers latins*, Édition critique de Dom Robert Weber, 1953
PIH	*Sancti Hieronymi Psalterium Iuxta Hebraeos*, Édition critique de Dom Henri de Sainte Marie, 1954
(OL)	(*Bibliorum Sacrorum*, Tomus ii, P. Sabatier, Ed., 1743, also consulted for Old Latin)
Targ	*Hagiographa Chaldaice* (תרגום כתובים), Paulus de Lagarde, Ed., 1873 (Pardes, מקראות גדולות, vol. x, New York, 1951, also consulted)
Syr	*The Peshitta Psalter*, William Emery Barnes, Ed., 1904 *Libri Veteris Testamenti Apocryphi*, Paulus de Lagarde, Ed., 1861

ABBREVIATIONS AND SIGNS

et om.	et omnes	In reference only to the above-listed editions of the witnesses. *Et al.* is used in those instances where the translations in the ancient versions, for idiomatic reasons, do not clearly indicate the 'Vorlage'. *Et om.* and *et rel.* are used where there seems to be no such doubt, but, even then, refer only to the editions of witnesses consulted.
et rel.	et reliqui	
et al.	et alii	
hebr.	hebraici	
>	is lacking in	
+	adds	
N.B.	*Nota bene*	

In the transcription few signs are needed:

אׄ	highly probable reading
א֯	uncertain reading
[ ]	lacuna
*	scribal dot

FRAGMENTS A, B, C I. PSS 101^{1-8} 102^{1-2}

(PL. III)

101^{1}]]שׁפט אשירה לכה[ ]𐤅̊𐤄 אזמרה
2]]יׄ תבוא לי אתהל[ ] בתום לבבי
] 3]עינׄי דבר בלׄ[ ]עׄשה
]]יׄ 4לבב[[
] 5 [
]] ורחב ל[6]אמני
]]בת עמדי הׄ[ ]רתני
7]] בקרב ביתי [ ] לוׄא
]] עינׄי 8לבקרים א[ ]תׄ
]]𐤉̇𐤄𐤅𐤄 כול פׄ[ ]ל[[
102^{1}] [לעני כי יעטו[[
2]]שׁמעה תפל[[

L. 2 (101^{2}) לי: אלי MT *et al.* (haplography? Budde, Gunkel לי).

Frags. A, B, C I. Aside from orthographical considerations MT is indicated for the lacunae.

FRAGMENT C II. PSS 102^{18-29} 103 (?$104)^{1}$

(PL. III)

תולעת הערער ולוא [19 [
אחרון ועם נברא יהלל 𐤉̇] 20 [
𐤉𐤄𐤅𐤄 משמים אל האר] 21 [
[ ]תח בני תמותה 22 לספר בצ] [
בירושלים 23 בהקבץ עמים] [
𐤉𐤄𐤅𐤄 24 כי ענה בדרך [25 [
תעלני בחצי ימי בדור ד̇] 26 [
נוסדה ומעשי ידיכה ש̇] 27 [
וכולם כבגד יבלו וכלבוש̇] 28 [
ושנותיכה לוא יתמו 29 בני] [
[ ]לדו̇ר
[103^{1}]ר̊כי נפשי את 𐤉̇] [

L. 1 (102^{18}) תולעת: תפלת MT *et om.*
L. 3 (102^{20}) הארץ: ארץ MT *et rel. hebr.*
L. 6 (102^{24}) כי > MT *et rel.*
L. 8 (102^{26}) נוסדה: יסדת MT *et om.*
L. 8 (102^{26}) ומעשי 1 ms Ken LXX Vulg PR Targ: ומעשה MT Σ *et rel.*
L. 9 (102^{27}) וכלבוש LXX Lat Syr: כלבוש MT.

L. 11 (102^{29}) לדור > MT PIH Targ Syr. (LXX εἰς τὸν αἰῶνα, Vulg *in saeculum* var: *in aeternum*, PR *in saeculum saeculi*. N.B.: לפניך > LXX Vulg PR.) לדויד as in 4QPs[b]?

Frag. C II. Aside from orthographical considerations MT is indicated for the lacunae.

FRAGMENT D. PS 109^{21-31}

(PL. III)

[ ]מכה כי טוב
[22]י חלל בקרבי
23[24]כי כשלו מצום
[25]לה̊ם יראוני
[26]ושיעני
[27]אתה עשיתה
28[ ]כה ישמח
29[ ]ם 30אודה
[31]כי עמד

L. 6 (109^{27}) אתה [יהוה]: אתה יהוה MT. Lacuna indicates juxtaposition?

L. 9 (109^{31}) עמד LXX Vulg PR Syr: יעמד MT *et al.* (Grk *παρέστη*, Vulg PR *adstetit*, PIH *stabit.*)

Frag. D. Aside from orthographical considerations MT is indicated for the lacunae, and Ps 105 could have followed directly.

COLUMN I. PS 105$^{25-45}$

(PL. IV)

[25]לבם לשנוא

[26]רון אשר בחר

[27 28]ה֯ חושך

[ ]ר֯ם ?29 שם

[30]רצה ארצם

[31]נ֯ים בכול

[32 33]ך גפנם

[34]וילק ואין

[35]ד֯מתם

[36 37]ת עמו

[38]ת֯ם כי

[39] לילה

[40 41]ור ויזובו

[42]א֯ברהם

[43] 44ויתן

[45]ר֯ ישמורו

L. 4 (105^{28}) [?דב]רם: דבריו MT *et om.* (Lacuna may support independent readings and addenda, or may only indicate scribal erasure or poor writing surface avoided. Cf. l. 15.)

L. 4 (105^{29}) שם: הפך MT *et om.* (Text preceding and following highly uncertain.)

L. 5 (105^{30}) ש[רצה: שרץ MT *et al.*

L. 10 (105^{37}) [?ויוצא א]ת עמו cf. v. 43: ויוציאם MT *et om.*

L. 15 (105^{44}) N.B.: erasure (of לתת?) before ויתן.

Col. I. Aside from l. 4 specifically, and orthographical considerations generally, MT is indicated for the lacunae, and Ps 146 would have followed directly.

COLUMN II. PSS $146^{9-?-10}$ 148^{1-12}

(PL. IV)

יתום ואלמנה יעודד ודרך] [

מ𐤉𐤄𐤅𐤄 כול הארץ ממנ] [

בהודעו לכול מעשיו ברא] [

גבורותיו 10 ימלוך 𐤉𐤄𐤅𐤄] [

ודור הללויה

148 1 הללו 𐤉𐤄𐤅𐤄 משמים הלל] 2 [

כול מלאכיו הללוהו כול צבא] 3 [

הללוהו כול כוכבי אור 4 הללו] [

אשר מעל לשמים 5 הללו את] [

צוה ונבראו 6 ויעמידם לע] [

יעבור 7 הללו את 𐤉𐤄𐤅𐤄 מ] [

תהומות 8 אש וברד שלג וק] [

עושה דברו 9 ההרים וכול] [

ארזים 10 החיה וכול בהמה] 11 [

אר̊] [וכול לאומים שרים ו] 12 [

] [לות זקנים עם נע] 13 [

Ll. 2–4 (146^{9-10}) מיהוה כול הארץ . . . גבורותיו > MT *et om.* For ll. 1–2 see Ps 33^{8} and for ll. 3–4 see perhaps (?) Ps 145^{10-12}.

L. 6 (Ps 148) Superscription > Q. Cf. PR PIH.

L. 6 (148^{1}) הללו יהוה משמים : הללו את יהוה מן השמים MT *et al. hebr.*

L. 9 (148^{4}) לשמים : השמים MT *et al. hebr.*

L. 9 (148^{5}) הללו : יהללו MT *et om.*

L. 15 (148^{11}) לאומים Ken: לאמים MT.

Col. II. Aside from ll. 1–4 specifically, and orthographical considerations generally, MT is indicated for the lacunae, and Ps 120 would have followed directly to complete the column.

COLUMN III. PSS 121$^{1-8}$ 122$^{1-9}$ 123$^{1-2}$

(PL. IV)

121 1שיר המעלות אשא עיני אל ההרים מאין יבוא [ ]
[ ]2עזרי מעם 𐤉𐤄𐤅𐤄 עושה שמים וארץ 3אל יתן ל[ ]
[ ]לכה ואל []נום שומרכה 4הנה לוא ינום ולוא יישן[ ]
[ ]שׂראל 5בלילה 𐤉𐤄𐤅𐤄 שומרכה צלכה על יד ימינכה 6יומׄ[ ]
[ ]מש לוא יככה וירח בלילה 7𐤉𐤄𐤅𐤄 ישומרכה מכו[ ] יש[ ]
[ ]תׄ נפשכה 8ישמור צאתכה ובואכה מעתה ועד עׄ[ ]
122 1שיר המעלות לדויד ש[ ]
[ ]בית 𐤉𐤄𐤅𐤄 נלך 2עומדות היו רגלי בשעריך [ ]
[ ]ושלים 3ירושלים הבנוה כעיר שחברה לו 4שמה[ ]
?] עדת ישראל להודות לשם 𐤉𐤄𐤅𐤄 5כי שׄ[ ]
[ ]משׄפט כסא לבית דויד 6שאלו שלום ירוש[ ]
[ ]והביך 7יהי שלום בחילך ושלוה בארמונותיך [8]
[ ]רׄעי אדברה שלום בך 9למען בית 𐤉𐤄𐤅𐤄 אלו[ ]
[ ]טובה לך [ ]
[123 1]דויד למעלות[ ]ליכה נׄ[ש]י [ ]ני היושב בשמ[2]
[ ]עבדים אל[ ]יהם[ ]עׄ[ ]נׄיׄ[ ]

L. 1 (121^{1}) המעלות Ken: למעלות MT.

L. 2 (121^{2}) מעם—the ע is inserted above the ם.

L. 3 (121^{3}) ואל Ken LXX PR Vulg PIH Syr: אל MT *et al.*

L. 4 (121^{5}) בלילה > MT *et rel.* N.B.: destructive worm tracing at this point in ll. 3–5.

L. 4 (121^{5}) יהוה^{2} MT *et om.* > Q. N.B.: space left blank.

L. 6 (121^{8}) יהוה MT *et al.* > Q.

L. 8 (122^{2}) רגלי Syr: רגלינו MT *et rel.* N.B.: possible erasure of יר at end of line.

L. 9 (122^{3}) הבנויה—the י is inserted above the ו.

L. 9 (122^{3}) לו: לה יחדו MT *et al.* N.B.: לו in reference also to Jerusalem in iv 4: Ps 125^{2}.

L. 9 (122^{4}) שמה Syr: ששם MT *et al.*

L. 10 (122^{4}) עלו שבטים שבטי יה MT > Q?

L. 10 (122^{4}) עדת ישראל (Σ ἐκκλησία): עדות לישראל MT *et al.*

L. 11 (122^{5}) כסא: כסאות MT *et om.*

L. 11 (122^{6}) N.B.: erasure of *shin*, *'alef*, and following letter.

L. 12 (122^{7}) ושלוה Ken de Rossi LXX PR Vulg Syr: שלוה MT PIH Targ.

L. 13 (122^{8}) (אדברה־)נא MT *et al.* > Q.

L. 14 (122^{9}) טובה: טוב MT *et al. hebr.*

L. 15 (123^{1}) [ל]דויד למעלות: שיר המעלות MT *et al.* PIH (mss) David.

L. 15 (123^{1}) נֿש[את]י—the ש is inserted above the א.

L. 15 (123^{1}) את MT Targ > Q Ken.

L. 15 (123^{1}) היושב 1 ms Ken: הישבי MT *et al.*

Col. III. Aside from ll. 8–11 specifically, and orthographical considerations generally, MT is indicated for the lacunae, and Ps 124 would have followed directly. N.B.: right margin irregular at ll. 6–13, and fragments of l. 16 have adhered to the bottom of Col. II.

COLUMN IV. PSS 124^{7-8} 125^{1-5} 126^{1-6} 127^{1}

(PL. V)

] [נ͏ׄמלטנו 8עוזרנו בשם יהוה עושה
] [
125^{1}] [הבוטחים ביהוה כהר ציון שלוא
] [שב 2ירושלים הרים סביב לו יהוה
] [עׄתה ועד עולם 3כי לוא ינוח שבט הרשע
] [דׄיקים למען לוא ישלחו הצדיקים בעולתה
4] [בׄה יהוה לטובים ולישרים בלב 5עקלקולות
] [ה את כול פועלי און שלום על ישראל
126^{1}שיר המעלות בשוב יהוה
] [היינו כחלוׄמים 2אז ימלא שחוק פינו ולשוננו
] [אׄמרו בגויים הגדיל יהוה לעשות עם
3] [יׄל יהוה לעשות עמנו היינו שמחים
4] [וה את שבותינו כאפיקים בנגב 5הזורעים
] [הׄ יקצורו 6הלוך ילך ובכו נושאי משך הזרע
] [נׄה נושאי אלומותו
127^{1}] [לשלומהׄ אׄ[ ]ה לוא [ ]בנה[ ]תׄ שוא

L. 1 (124^{7}) N.B.: a trace of the superscribed second *nun* of אנחנו?

L. 3 (125^{1}) שלוא: לא MT *et rel.*

L. 4 (125^{2}) לו: לה MT *et al. hebr.* N.B.: לו in reference also to Jerusalem in iii 9: Ps 122^{3}.

L. 4 (125^{2}) יהוה: ויהוה MT *et om.* Haplography?

L. 7 (125^{4}) בלב 4QPs^{e} LXX Lat: בלבותם MT *et rel.*

L. 7 (125^{5}) והמטים MT *et om.* > Q 4QPs^{e}.

L. 7 (125^{5}) עקלקולות: עקלקלותם MT Σ *et al.* But suffix > LXX Vulg PR. N.B.: 4QPs^{e} has עקלקולים with ת inserted over the ם.

L. 8 (125^{5}) כול > MT *et om.*

L. 8 (125^{5}) און Ken: האון MT *et al. hebr.* (Cf. xxiii 5: Ps 141^{9b}.)

L. 10 (126^{1}) כחלומים LXX Vulg PR Targ (cf. Syr): כחלמים MT *Ά Σ E′* PIH. (*Ἑβρ — χαωλεμιμ.*) Read stative חלימים? N.B.: erasures at end of line. לשונינו? Cf. Ken.

L. 13 (126^{4}) שבותינו Ken: שבותנו MT ktb, שביתנו qere'.

L. 14 (126^{6}) ילך ובכו נושאי (cf. 1 ms Ken): ילכו ובכו נושאי (Q erasure?) LXX PR Vulg: ילך ובכה נושא MT *et al. hebr.* *Σ E′* PIH Targ Syr.

L. 15 (126^{6}) נושאי 1Q11:1 LXX PIH: נשא MT *et rel.*

Col. IV. Aside from orthographical considerations MT is indicated for the lacunae, and Ps 128 would have followed directly.

COLUMN V. PSS 128^{4-6} 129^{1-8} 130^{1-8} 131^{1}

(PL. V)

ל̊[4]גבר ירא 𐤉𐤄𐤅𐤄 5יברככה אדוני
[ ]ים כול ימי חייכה 6וראה בנים
ל̊[ ]
129[1] ש[ ]רוני מנעורי יואמר נא ישראל 2רבות
[ ]א̊ יכולו לי 3על גבי חרשו רשעים
[ ]4א̊דוני צדיק קצץ עבות רשעים 5יבושו
[ ]נאי ציון 6יהיו כחציר גגות שקדמת שלף
יב[7]צ̊ר וחוצנו מעמר 8שלוא אמרו העוברים
ב̇ד[ ]לוהיכמ עליכם ברכנו אתכם בשם 𐤉𐤄𐤅𐤄
[ ] 130[1] שיר המעלות אדוני ממעמקים
[2]ע̊ה בקולי תהי נא אוזנכה קשובת לי
[3]מ̊ור יה אדוני מי יעמוד 4כי עמכה הסליחה
[5]𐤉̊ קותה נפשי לדברו הוחלתי 6הוחילי
[ ]ב̊וקר שומרים לבוקר 7יחל ישראל
[ ]ה̊חסד הרב עמו פדה 8הוא יפדה את
[ ]ו̊
131[1] [ ]𐤉̊𐤄[ ]ל̊[ ]

L. 1 (128^{5}) אדוני: יהוה MT *et al.*

L. 4 (129^{2}) רבות 1 ms Ken: רבת MT *et rel.*

L. 5 (129^{3}) רשעים LXX Vulg PR: חרשים MT 𝔄 Σ *et rel.*

L. 6 (129^{4}) [א]דוני: יהוה MT *et al.*

L. 8 (129^{8}) שלוא: ולא MT *et al.* (PIH *de quo non dixerunt.*)

L. 9 (129^{8}) [בד[רך ברכת? > MT.

L. 9 (129^{8}) [א]לוהיכמ > MT *et om.*

L. 9 (129^{8}) עליכם Ken (cf. LXX Lat Targ Syr): אליכם MT *et al.*

L. 10 (130^{1}) אדוני > MT *et om.* Juxtaposition?

L. 11 (130^{1-2}) [קראתי יהוה שמ[עה?]—reconstruction uncertain. There are tracings above the ה but they are indistinguishable.

L. 11 (130^{2}) תהי נא: תהיינה MT *et om.*

L. 11 (130^{2}) אוזנכה Ken (אזנך): אזניך MT *et rel.*

L. 11 (130^{2}) קשובת 3 mss Ken: קשבות MT *et rel.*

L. 11 (130^{2}) לי > MT *et om.*

L. 13 (130^{5}) לדברו 1 ms Ken LXX Vulg PR Syr (?): ולדברו MT 𝔄 PIH Targ (?).

L. 13 (130^{6}) הוחילי (cf. Pss $42^{6, 12}$ 43^{5}) > MT *et om.* (Grk ἤλπισεν, but הוחלתי of v. 5 > LXX.)

L. 15 (130^{7}) הרב, עֲמו פדה: והרבה עִמו פדות MT *et om.*

L. 15 (130^{8}) הוא Syr: והוא MT *et rel.*

L. 17 (131^{1}) Traces of this line have adhered to the bottom of Col. IV.

Col. V. Aside from ll. 1, 9, 11 and orthographical considerations MT is indicated for the lacunae, and Ps 132 would have followed directly.

COLUMN VI. PSS 132^{8-18} 119^{1-6}

(PL. VI)

למנוחתכה אתה וא[ ]ע֯ו֯ז֯כ֯ה֯ 9 כוהניכה ילבשו צדק וחסידיכה
ירננו 10 בעבור דויד עבדכה אל תשב   פני משיחכה 11 נשבע
𐤉𐤄𐤅𐤄 לדויד [ ]ל[ ] ישוב ממנה כי מפרי בטנכה   אשית
על כסא לכה 12 [ ]שמ֯[]ר֯ו בניכה בריתי ועדוותי זה
אלמדם גם בנ[ ]ם עודי עד יעלו לכסא לכה 13 כי בחר
𐤉𐤄𐤅𐤄 בציון א[ ] למושב לו 14 זואת מנוחתי עדי עד פה
אשב כי אוית[15] ב֯ר֯ך֯ אברך אביוניה אשביע
לחם 16 וכוהניה א[ ]ש֯ה יש֯ע֯ וחסידיה ירננו 17 שם אצמיח
קרן לדויד ער֯[ ]נ֯ר למשיחי 18 אויביו אלביש בושת ועליו
יציץ נזרו֯ [ ] [
119 1 אשרי תמי[ ]הולכים בתורת 𐤉𐤄𐤅𐤄
2 אשרי[ ]עת ידורשוה
3 אף ל[ ]ו הלכו
4 את [ ]ור מואדה
5 אחל[ ]מתכה
6 אז ל[ ]ל מצוותיכה

L. 2 (132^{10}) N.B.: erasure (of תשב?) after תשב.
L. 3 (132^{11}) כי > MT *et al.*
L. 4 (132^{11}) על כסא: לכסא MT *et rel. hebr.*
L. 4 (132^{12}) זה 1 ms Ken: זוֹ MT.
L. 5 (132^{12}) עודי: עדי MT *et rel. hebr.* (But cf. *infra* l. 6.)
L. 5 (132^{12}) יעלו: ישבו MT *et om.*
L. 8 (132^{16}) רנן MT *et om.* > Q.
L. 10 (132^{18}) נזרו MT 𝔄 PIH Targ: נזרי LXX Vulg PR Syr.
L. 12 (119^{2}) עת 1 ms Ken: לב MT *et om.* (Cf. vii 6: Ps 119^{20}.)
L. 12 (119^{2}) ידורשוה: ידרשוהו MT *et om.*
L. 15 (119^{5}) [?א]מתכה: חקיך MT *et om.* (Müller, Baethgen, *et al.* אמרתך.)
Col. VI. Aside from orthographical considerations MT is indicated for the lacunae.

COLUMN VII. PS 119^{15-28}

(PL. VI)

15 בפקודיכה אשיחה ואביטה אורחותיכה
16 בחוקיכה אשתעשע לוא אשכח דבריכה

17 גמור על עבדכה ואחיה ואשמורה דבריכה
18 גל עיני ואביטה נפלאות מתורותיכה
19 גר אנוכי בארץ אל תסתר ממני מצוותיכה
20 גרשה נפשי לתאבה אל משפטיכה בכול עת
21 גערתה זדים ארורים השוגים ממצוותיכה
22 גול מעלי חרפה ובוז כי עדוותיכה נצרתי
23 גם ישבו שרים בי נדברו עבדכה ישיח בחוקיכה
24 גם עדוותיכה שעשׂוׂעיׂ[ ]אנשי עצתי

25 דבקה לעפר נפֿ[ ]
26 דרכי ספרתי ותֿ[ ]ה
27 דרך פקודׄיכה הֿ[ ]לאותיכה
28 דלפה נפשי מ[ ]כֿה

L. 2 (119^{16}) בחוקיכה: בחקתיך MT *et al. hebr.*

L. 2 (119^{16}) דבריכה MT qere' Ken de Rossi Grk Lat Targ Syr: דברך MT ktb.

L. 3 (119^{17}) גמור 4QPs^h Ken: גמל MT *et al.* (Cf. Pss 57^3 138^8.)

L. 3 (119^{17}) ואחיה 4QPs^h Ken (cf. OL Syr): אחיה MT *et rel.*

L. 3 (119^{17}) דבריכה MT qere' Ken de Rossi Grk Lat Syr Targ: דברך MT ktb.

L. 4 (119^{18}) מתורותיכה Ken: (מ)תורתך MT *et rel.*

L. 6 (119^{20}) גרשה: גרסה MT *et al.*

L. 8 (119^{22}) גול (qal impv. of גלל): גל MT. Cf. versions.

L. 13 (119^{27}) פקודיכה—the י is inserted above the כ. Cf. Ken for sing.

Ll. 10–14 (119^{24-28}) Aside from orthographical considerations MT is indicated for the lacunae.

COLUMN VIII. PS 119^{37-49}

(PL. VII)

37 העבר עיני מראות שוא כדברכה חונני
38 הקם לעבדכה אמרתכה אשר ליראתכה
39 העבר חרפתי אשר יגרתי כי משפטיכה טובים
40 הנה תאבתי לפקודיכה בצדקתכה חונני

41 ויבואוני חסד 𐤉𐤄𐤅𐤄 תשועתכה כאמרתכה
42 ואענה חורפי דבר כי בטחתי בדברכה
43 ואל תצל מפי דבר אמת עד מואדה כי לדבריכה יחלתי
44 ואשמורה תורתכה תמיד ועד 45 ואתהלכה ברחוביה
כי פקודיכה דרשתי
46 ואדברה בעדוותיכׄהׄ [ ]גׄד מלכים ולוא אבוש
47 ואשתעשעה במ[ ]שׄר אהבתי
48 ואשא כפי אל מצוו[ ]ר אהבתי ואשישה בחוקיכה

49 זכורה דבריכה[ ]לׄ[ ] יחלתני

L. 1 (119^{37}) כדברכה: בדרכך MT ktb Grk Lat: בדרכיך MT qere' Ken de Rossi Syr: בדברך Ken de Rossi Targ (Olshausen *et al.*).

L. 1 (119^{37}) חונני (cf. xii 5 xiii 5 xix 14 and *supra* Introduction): חיני MT *et om.*

L. 4 (119^{40}) חונני (cf. *supra* l. 1): חיני MT *et om.*

L. 5 (119^{41}) ויבואוני חסד: ויבואוני חסדך MT ktb LXX Vulg: ויבואוני חסדיך MT qere' Ken PIH Targ.

L. 6 (119^{42}) ואענה—the א is inserted above the ע.

L. 7 (119^{43}) לדבריכה: למשפטך MT ktb Targ: למשפטיך MT qere' Ken de Rossi Grk Lat Targ Syr.

L. 8 (119^{44}) לעולם MT *et om.* > Q.

L. 8 (119^{45}) ברחוביה: ברחבה MT *et om.* N.B.: (1) v. 45 alone in 11QPs 119 does not begin at right margin, but follows immediately on v. 44; (2) Syr v. 45 (cf. also Syr v. 118) also follows immediately on v. 44 in Barnes's edition; (3) cf., however, 1QPs 119, *DJD I*, p. 70.

L. 12 (119^{48}) ואשישה (Syr?): ואשיחה MT *et rel.*

L. 13 (119^{49}) דבריכה LXX[LUC] *Θ O′*: דבר MT *Ά* PIH Targ (cf. Vulg): דברך LXX Vulg PR Syr.

Ll. 10–13 (119^{46-49}) Aside from orthographical considerations MT is indicated for the lacunae.

COLUMN IX. PS 119^{59-73}

(PL. VII)

59 חשבתי דרכי ואשיבה רגלי אל עדוותיכה
60 חשתי ולוא התמהמהתי לשמור מצוותיכה
61 חבלי רשעים עודוני תורתכה לוא שכחתי
62 חצות לילה אקום להודות לכה על משפטי צדקכה
63 חבר אני לכול אשר יראוכה ולשומרי פקודיכה
64 חסדכה 𐤉𐤄𐤅𐤄 מלאה הארץ חוקכה למדני

65 טוב עשיתה עם עבדכה 𐤉𐤄𐤅𐤄 כדברכה
66 טוב טעם ודעת למדני כי במצוותיכה האמנתי
67 טרם אענה אני שוגג ועתה אמרתכה שמרתי
68 טוב אתה אדוני ומטיב למדני חוקיכה
69 טפלו עלי שקר זדים אני בכֿול ל[ ] אצורה פקודיכה
70 טפש כחלב לבם אני תורתכ[שֿעֿ[ ]ועי
71 טוב לי כי עניתני למען אלמֿ[ ]יכה
72 טוב לי תורת פיכה מאלףֿ[ ]
73]]כֿהֿ

L. 1 (119^{59}) **ואשיבה** N.B.: possible erasure (of **ת**?) under the **ב**.

L. 3 (119^{61}) **עודוני** MT qere' Ken de Rossi: **עודני** MT ktb.

L. 6 (119^{64}) **חוקכה**: **חקיך** MT *et om.*

L. 10 (119^{68}) **אדוני** LXX PR Syr > MT *et rel.*

L. 12 (119^{70}) **שע[ש]ועי** 1 ms Ken *Ά Σ* Targ (cf. Ps $119^{24, 77, 92, 143, 174}$): **שעשעתי** MT *et al.* (E.g. LXX *ἐμελέτησα*, PIH *delectabor.*)

L. 13 (119^{71}) **עניתני** 1 ms Ken LXX *Θ* Vulg PR (cf. Ps 88^{8}): **עֻניתי** MT *et al.*

L. 14 (119^{72}) ? **מאלף** Targ (cf. Gen 20^{16}, II Sam 18^{12}, Isa 7^{23}, Cant 8^{11}): **מאלפי** MT *et al.* Q?

Ll. 11–15 (119^{69-73}) Aside from orthographical considerations MT is indicated for the lacunae.

COLUMN X. PS 119^{82-96}

(PL. VIII)

82 כלתה עיני לאמרתכה לאמור מתי תנחמני
83 כי עשיתני כנאוד בקיטור חסדכה לוא שכחתי
84 כמה ימי עבדכה מתי תעשה ברודפי משפט
85 כרו לי זידים שחת אשר לוא כתורתכה
86 כול מצוותיכה אמונה שקר רדפוני עוזרני
87 כמעט כלוני מארץ ואני לוא עזבתי פקודיכה
88 כחסדכה חונני ואשמורה עדוות פיכה

89 לעולם יהוה דברכה נצב בשמים
90 לדור ודור אמונתכה כוננתה ארץ ותעמד
91 למשפטיכה עמדו היום כי הכול עבדי̊כה
92 לולי תורתכה שעשועי אז אבדתי בעווני
93 לעולם לוא אשכח פקודיכה כי במה חייתני
94 לכה אני הושיעני כי פקודיכה דרשתי
95 לי קוו רשעים לאבדני עדוותיכה אתבונן
96 לכול תכלה ראיתי קץ רחבה מצותכ[ ] מואדה

L. 1 (119^{82}) כלתה (cf. v. 81): כלו MT *et om.*
L. 2 (119^{83}) עשיתני: הייתי MT *et om.*
L. 2 (119^{83}) חסדכה: חקיך MT *et om.*
L. 4 (119^{85}) שחת 1 ms Ken: שׂיחות MT PIH *et al.*: שִׂיחות LXX (ἀδολεσχίας) Vulg PR.
L. 6 (119^{87}) מארץ (Gunkel): בארץ MT *et om.*
L. 7 (119^{88}) חונני: חיני MT *et om.* Cf. viii 1.
L. 7 (119^{88}) עדוות LXX Vulg: עדוּת MT PIH Syr (?).
L. 9 (119^{90}) (?) ותעמֵד Syr: ותעמֹד MT *et rel.*
L. 10 (119^{91}) עבדיכה LXX *Ἀ Σ Θ* Targ: עבדוך Lat (?). N.B.: v. 91 > Syr.
L. 11 (119^{92}) בעווני 1 ms Ken: בעניי MT *et rel.*

COLUMN XI. PS 119^{105-20}

(PL. VIII)

105 נר לרגלי דבריכה אור לנתיבותי

106 נשבעתי ואקימה לעשות משפט צדקכה

107 נעויתי עד מואדה 𐤉𐤄𐤅𐤄 כאמרתכה חונני

108 נדבות פי רצה 𐤉𐤄𐤅𐤄 ממשפטיכה למדני

109 נפשי בכפי תמיד תורתכה לוא שכחתי

110 נתנו רשעים פח לי אני פקודיכה לוא תעיתי

111 נחלתי עדוותיכה לעולם   ששון לבי המה

112 נטיתי לבי לעשות חוקיכה לעולם עקב

113 סעפים שנאתי תורתכה אהבתי

114 סתרי ומגני אתה לדבריכה יחלתי

115 סורו ממני מרעים ואצורה מצות אלוהי

116 סמכני כאמרתכה ואחיה ואל תבישני ממשברי

117 סעדני ואושעה ואשא חוקיכה תמיד

118 סליתה כול שוגים מחוקיכה כי שקר תרמיתם

119 סיגים חשבתי כול רשעי ארץ על כן אהבתי כול עדוותיכה

120 סמר מפחד[ ]בשרי וממשפטיכה יראתי

L. 1 (119^{105}) דבריכה MT qere' Ken de Rossi Targ: דברך MT ktb LXX *Ά* Lat Syr.

L. 1 (119^{105}) אור: ואור MT *et om.*

L. 1 (119^{105}) לנתיבותי LXX Vulg PR Syr: לנתיבָתי MT *et rel. hebr.* PIH Targ.

L. 2 (119^{106}) לעשות: לשמר MT *et om.*

L. 2 (119^{106}) משפט 2 mss Ken: משפטֵי MT *et rel.* N.B.: erasure of *yod.*

L. 3 (119^{107}) נעויתי: נעניתי MT *et om.*

L. 3 (119^{107}) כאמרתכה חונני: חיני כדברך MT *et om.* For חונני cf. viii 1, &c. For כאמרתך cf. Gunkel (and LXX *λόγιον*?).

L. 4 (119^{108}) רצה 2 mss Ken: רצה־נא MT *et rel.*?

L. 4 (119^{108}) ממשפטיכה Syr: ומשפטיך MT *et rel.*

L. 5 (119^{109}) תורתכה: ותורתך MT *et om.*

L. 6 (119^{110}) אני > MT *et rel.* N.B.: אני aural error for ומ׳? Cf. xvi 4, 5.

L. 6 (119^{110}) פקודיכה: ומפקודיך MT *et om.*

L. 7 (119^{111}) N.B.: erasure of כי (of MT *et. om.*) with scribal dots (?).

L. 9 (119^{113}) תורתכה: ותורתך MT *et om.*

L. 10 (119^{114}) לדבריכה 1 ms Ken LXX^LUC A^: לדברך MT *et rel.*

L. 11 (119^{115}) מצות sing.?: מצות pl. MT *et om.* N.B.: if מצות here is plural it is orthographically unique in Q.

L. 12 (119^{116}) ממשברי: משברי MT *et rel. hebr.*

L. 13 (119^{117}) ואשא: ואשעה MT *et rel. hebr.*: ואשתעשע Grk Vulg PR Syr Targ. (PIH *delectabor.*)

L. 13 (119^{117}) חוקיכה: בחקיך MT *et om.*

L. 15 (119^{119}) חשבתי LXX Vulg PR: השבת MT *Θ E′* Targ: חשבת Ken de Rossi *Ά Σ* PIH. N.B.: v. 119 > Syr.

L. 15 (119^{119}) על כן (Targ מטול היכנא): לכן MT 5QPs 119 *et al.*

L. 15 (119^{119}) כול[2] > MT 5QPs 119 *et rel.*

COLUMN XII. PS 119 128–42

(PL. IX)

128 על כן פקודי כול ישרתי כול אורח שקר שנאתי

129 פלגי נפת עדוותיכה על כן נצרתם נפשי
130 פתח דבריכה והאר מבין פותאים
131 פי פערתי ואשאפה למצוותיכה תאבתי
132 פנה אלי וחונני כמשפט לאוהבי שמכה
133 פעמי הכן לאמרתכה ואל תשלט בי כול און
134 פדני מעשק אדם ואשמורה פקודיכה
135 פניכה האר בעבדכה ולמדני את חוקיכה
136 פלגי מים ירדו עיני על כי לוא שמרו תורתכה

137 צדיק אתה וישרים משפטיכה
138 צויתה צדק עדוותיכה ואמונה מואדה
139 צמתתני קנאתי כי שכחו דבריכה צרי
140 צרופה אמרתכה מואדה עבדכה אהבה
141 צעיר אנוכי ונבזה פקודיכה לוא שכחתי
142 [ ]ות[ ]דקות עולם ותורתך אמת

L. 1 (119^{128}) פקודי כול 1 ms Ken Vulg PIH: כל פקודי כל MT *et rel.*

L. 2 (119^{129}) פלגי נפת: פלאות MT *et om.* (Cf. *infra* l. 9.)

L. 3 (119^{130}) והאר Syr: יאיר MT *et rel.*

L. 3 (119^{130}) פותאים: פתיים MT *et al.* (Cf. xviii 3–4 and 1QHf 15^{4}.)

L. 4 (119^{131}) MT כי > Q 2 mss Ken Syr.

L. 4 (119^{131}) תאבתי: יאבתי MT *hapax.* (Cf. viii 4 xiv 4: Ps $119^{40, 174}$.)

L. 5 (119^{132}) וחונני 1 ms Ken: וחנני MT.

L. 6 (119^{133}) לאמרתכה 3 mss de Rossi: באמרתך MT PIH Targ Syr: כאמרתך Ken de Rossi LXX Vulg PR.

L. 9 (119^{136}) כי > MT *et rel. hebr.*

L. 10 (119^{137}) וישרים: וישר MT.

L. 13 (119^{140}) עבדכה: ועבדך MT *et om.* N.B.: the ד is inserted above the ב and כ.

L. 15 (119^{142}) צ]דקות[צדק]ות[: ?צדקתך צדק MT *et om.*

L. 15 (119^{142}) עולם: לעולם MT *et al.*

COLUMN XIII. PS 119^{150-64}

(PL. IX)

150 קרבו רודפי זמה מתורתכה רחקו

151 קרוב אתה יהוה וכול מצוותיכה אמת

152 קדם ידעתי מדעתכה כי לעולם יסדתני

153 ראה עוניי וחלצני תורתכה לוא שכחתי

154 ריבה ריבי וגאלני לאמרתכה חיני

155 רחוק מרשעים ישועה כי חוקיכה לוא דרשו

156 רחמיכה רבים יהוה כמשפטיכה חונני

157 רבים רודפי וצרי מעדוותיכה לוא נטיתי

158 ראיתי בוגדים ואתקוטטה אשר אמרתכה
לוא שמרו

159 ראה כי פקודיכה אהבתי יהוה כאמרתכה חונני

160 רו֯[ ] דבריכה אמת ולעולם כול משפט צדק

161 שרים רדפוני חנום ומדבריכה פחד לבי

162 שש אנוכי על אמרתכה ממוצא שלל רב

163 שק֯[ ]תי ואתעבה ותורתכה אהבתי

164 [ ]ל[ ]שׂ֯פ֯ט֯י

L. 3 (119^{152}) מדעתכה: מעדתיך MT *et om.* Cf. 1QH i 21 xv 12.

L. 3 (119^{152}) יסדתני: יסדתם MT *et om.*

L. 4 (119^{153}) עוניי: עניי MT. (Cf. Introduction on *qameṣ ḥaṭuf.*)

L. 4 (119^{153}) MT *et om.* כי > Q. Haplography?

L. 5 (119^{154}) ריבה N.B.: the ה is inserted above the line after ב.

L. 5 (119^{154}) חיני N.B.: the single instance in $11QPs^a$ where Q = MT חיני. Cf. *infra* ll. 7 and 11 and Introduction.

L. 6 (119^{155}) ישועה is inserted above the line.

L. 7 (119^{156}) חוני: חיני MT *et om.*

L. 11 (119^{159}) כאמרתכה: כחסדך MT PIH Targ: בחסדך LXX *et al.*

L. 11 (119^{159}) חונני: חיני MT *et om.*

L. 12 (119^{160}) דבריכה 1 ms Ken LXX Lat: דברך MT *et rel.*

L. 12 (119^{160}) צדק: צדקך MT *et om.*

L. 13 (119^{161}) חנום: חנם MT *et al.* Cf. Introduction.

L. 13 (119^{161}) ומדבריכה MT ktb LXX Lat: ומדברך MT qere' Targ Syr.

L. 14 (119^{162}) ממוצא: כמוצא MT *et om.*

L. 15 (119^{163}) ותורתכה Ken Syr LXX (δὲ) Vulg PR (?): תורתך MT *et rel.*

Ll. 12, 15–16 ($119^{160, 163-4}$) Aside from orthographical considerations MT is indicated for the lacunae.

COLUMN XIV. PSS 119[171–6] 135[1–9]

(PL. X)

171 תבענה שפתי תהלה לכה כי תלמדני חוקיכה
172 תענה לשוני אמרתכה כי כול מצוותיכה צדק
173 תהי ידכה לעוזרני כי פקודיכה בחרתי
174 תאבתי לישועתכה 𐤉𐤄𐤅𐤄 תורתכה שעשועי
175 תחי נפשי ותהללכה וֹמֹשפטיכה יעוזרני
176 תעיתי כשה אובד בקש עבדכה כי עדוותיכה לוא שכחתי

135[1] הללו עבדי 𐤉𐤄𐤅𐤄 הללו את שם 𐤉𐤄𐤅𐤄 הללו יה
2 ורוממו יה שעומדים בבית
𐤉𐤄𐤅𐤄 בחצרות בית אלוהינו ובתוכך ירושלים
3 הללו את 𐤉𐤄𐤅𐤄 כי טוב זמרו שמו כי נעים 4 כי יעקוב
בחר לו וישראל לסגולה לו 5 אני ידעתי כי גדול 𐤉𐤄𐤅𐤄
ואלוהינו מכול אלוהים 6 אשר חפץ 𐤉𐤄𐤅𐤄 עשה
בשמים ובארץ לעשות יעשה אין כיה אין כ𐤉𐤄𐤅𐤄
ואין שיעשה כמלך אלוהים בימים ובכול תֿהומות 7 מעלה
נשיאֿ[ ]קֿצֿה הארץ ברקים למטר עשה מוציא רוח
] 8]∘∘∘∘[9]ל[]

L. 1 (119[171]) לכה Syr > MT *et rel.*
L. 2 (119[172]) תענה: תען MT.
L. 3 (119[173]) לעוזרני: לעזרני MT. (Cf. Introduction on *qameṣ ḥaṭuf*.)
L. 4 (119[174]) תורתכה: ותורתך MT *et om.*
L. 5 (119[175]) ומשפטיכה MT qere' Ken LXX Lat: ומשפטך MT ktb Syr. N.B.: scribal dots over ו and מ!
L. 5 (119[175]) יעוזרני: יעזְרֻני MT qere' *et al.*: יעזרני MT ktb 1 ms Ken.
L. 6 (119[176]) עדוותיכה: מצותיך MT *et om.*
L. 7 (135[1]) N.B.: the three הללו phrases of v. 1 are inverted MT (C, B, A); Q = 2 mss Ken (clears ambiguity? Cf. LXX). Cf. Ps 113[1].
L. 8 (135[2]) ורוממו יה > MT *et rel.* (Cf. Ps 99[5, 9].) N.B.: poor writing surface skipped by scribe.
L. 9 (135[2]) ובתוכך ירושלים > MT *et rel.* Cf. Ps 116[19].
L. 10 (135[3]) את יהוה: ־יה MT.
L. 10 (135[3]) כי טוב Syr OL: כי טוב יהוה MT *et al.*
L. 10 (135[3]) שמו: לשמו MT *et om.*
L. 11 (135[4]) יה MT *et al.* > Q.
L. 11 (135[4]) וישראל Syr (?) Σ: ישראל MT *et al.*
L. 11 (135[4]) לסגולה לו LXX[LUC] O′ Σ (?) Vulg PR (*in possessionem sibi*): לסגלתו MT *et rel.*
L. 11 (135[5]) כי[1] MT *et om.* > Q.
L. 12 (135[5]) ואלוהינו Vulg PR: ואדנינו MT *et rel.*
L. 12 (135[6]) כל MT *et om.* > Q.
Ll. 13–14 (135[6]) לעשות . . . אלוהים (4QPs[n]–?) > MT *et rel.* N.B.: לעשות יעשה is the fragmentary reading in 4QPs[n].
L. 14 (135[6]) ובכול Ken de Rossi Syr LXX[B] Vulg PIH: וכל MT Targ: ובתהומות LXX PR.
Ll. 15–16 (135[7–9]) Aside from orthographical considerations MT is indicated for the lacunae.

COLUMN XV. PSS 135^{17-21} 136^{1-16}

(PL. X)

להם ולוא יאזינו ואין יש רוח בפיהם 18 כמוהם יהיו עושיהם וכול
אשר בטח בהם 19 בית ישראל ברכו את 𐤉𐤄𐤅𐤄 בית אהרון
ברכו את 𐤉𐤄𐤅𐤄 20 בית הלוי ברכו את 𐤉𐤄𐤅𐤄 יראי
𐤉𐤄𐤅𐤄 ברכו את 𐤉𐤄𐤅𐤄 21 יברככה 𐤉𐤄𐤅𐤄 מציון שוכן
ירושלים הללו יה
136 1 הודו ל𐤉𐤄𐤅𐤄 כי טוב כי לעולם חסדו 2 הודו לאלוהי האלוהים
כי לעולם חסדו 3 הודו לאדון האדונים כי לעולם חסדו
4 לעושה נפלאות לבדו כי לעולם חסדו 5 לעושה השמים
בתבונה כי לעולם חסדו 6 לרוקע הארץ על המים כי
לעולם חסדו 7 לעושה מאורות גדולים כי לעולם חסדו את
השמש וירח כי לעולם חסדו 8 את השמש לממשלות יום
כי לעולם חסדו 9 ירח וכוכבים לממשלות בלילה כי לעולם חסדו
10 למכה מצרים בבכוריהם כי לעולם חסדו 11 ויוציא ישראל
מתוכם כי לעולם חסדו 12 ביד חזקה ובאזרוע נטויה כי
לעולם חסדו 13 לגוזר ים סוף לגזרים כ֯י לעולם חסדו 14 והעבר
ישר֯אל בתוכו כי לעולם חסדו 15 נער פרעוה וחילו בים
[ ] ל֯[ ] 16 למ֯וליך עמו ב[ ]בר כ֯י ל[ ]ל[]

L. 1 (135^{17}) ואין 1 ms Ken Syr Targ: אף אין MT *et al.*

L. 1 (135^{18}) וכול Ken LXX Vulg PR Syr: כל MT PIH Targ *O′*.

Ll. 2–3 N.B.: poor writing surface avoided.

L. 2 (135^{18}) בטח qal perfect? Cf. Hex.

L. 4 (135^{21}) יברככה: ברוך MT *et om.* (Cf. xxviii 2: Ps 134^{3}.)

L. 7 (136^{3}) לאדון: לאדני MT *et al. hebr.* Targ.

L. 8 (136^{4}) גדלות MT *et om.* > Q.

Ll. 8–9 N.B.: poor writing surface avoided.

L. 10 (136^{7}) מאורות: אורים MT.

Ll. 10–11 ($136^{7 f.}$) את השמש . . . חסדו > MT *et rel.* (Cf. beginnings of vv. 8 and 9.) N.B.: erasure of ואת before second word of l. 11.

L. 11 (136^{8}) לממשלות 3 mss Ken (cf. MT v. 9): לממשלת MT *et al.* (Cf. Gen 1^{16}.)

L. 11 (136^{8}) יום Syr: ביום MT *et al. hebr.* Targ.

L. 12 (136^{9}) ירח: את הירח MT *et al. hebr.* Targ.

L. 14 (136^{12}) ובאזרוע: ובזרוע MT.

L. 16 (136^{15}) נער: ונער MT *et om.* LXX? Haplography?

Ll. 16–17 (136^{14-16}) Aside from orthographical considerations MT is indicated for the lacunae.

COLUMN XVI. PSS 136^{26} $118^{1(?), 15, 16, 8, 9, ?, 29}$ 145^{1-7}

(PL. XI)

כי לעולם חסדו $118^{1(?)}$ הודו ליהוה כי טוב כי לעולם חסדו 15 קול
רנה וישועה באהלי צדיקים ימין יהוה עשה חיל 16 ימין
יהוה רוממה ימין יהוה עשתה גבורה 8 טוב לבטוח
ביהוה מבטוח באדם 9 טוב לחסות ביהוה מבטוב
בנדיבים ? טוב לבטוב ביהוה מבטוח באלף עם 29 הודו
ליהוה כי טוב כי לעולם חסדו הללו יה

145^{1} תפלה לדויד ארוממכה יהוה אלוהי המלך
ואברכה שמכה לעולם ועד ברוך יהוה וברוך שמו
לעולם ועד 2 ברוך יום אברככה ואהללה שמכה לעולם ועד
ברוך יהוה ˹וברוך˺ שמו לעולם ועד 3 גדול יהוה ו˹מ˺הולל מואדה
לגדולתו אין חקר ברוך יהוה וברוך שמו לעולם ועד
4 דור לדור ישבחו מעשיכה וגבורתיכה יגידו ברוך יהוה
וברוך שמו לעולם ועד 5 הדר כבוד הודכה ידברו ונפלאותיכה
אשיח ברוך יהוה וברוך שמו לעולם ועד 6 ועזוז
נוראותיכה יואמרו וגדול˹ו˺תיכה אספר ברוך יהוה
[ ]מו לעולם ועד 7 זכר רב טובכה [ ]

L. 1 (136^{26}) כי לעולם חסדו—in all likelihood the end of Ps 136, but note the unusually small space interval before the addenda from Ps 118.

L. 1 ($118^{1(?)}$) הודו . . . חסדו—cf. *infra* ll. 5–6.

L. 3 (118^{16}) עשה חיל: עשתה גבורה MT. N.B.: all witnesses read vv. 15*b* and 16*b* the same, except that v. 16*b* > LXX^{א} PR. (LXX ἐποίησεν δύναμιν, PR PIH *fecit fortitudinem*, Syr Targ עבדת חילא.)

L. 3 (118^{8}) לבטוח: לחסות MT Targ *et al. hebr.*

L. 4 (118^{8}) מבטוח Q MT Targ *et al.* N.B.: in major witnesses the same infinitive is used in vv. 8*a* and 8*b*.

L. 4 (118^{9}) מבטוב: מבטוח MT Targ *et al.*

L. 5 (?) טוב? . . . עם > *om.*

L. 6 (118^{29}) הללו יה > MT *et rel.* Cf. LXX 118^{1}.

Ll. 6 f. N.B.: poor writing surfaces avoided.

L. 7 (145^{1}) תפלה: תהלה MT *et om.*

L. 7 (145^{1}) יהוה > MT *et rel.* N.B.: scribal error dots.

Ll. 8–9 (145^{1}) ברוך יהוה וברוך שמו לעולם ועד > MT *et rel.* N.B.: this refrain is constant to each verse of 11QPs 145 and unique to it.

L. 9 (145^{2}) ברוך: בכל MT *et om.* Cf. refrain.

L. 10 (145^{2}) וברוך is inserted above the line.

L. 10 (145^{3}) ומהולל N.B.: the מ is inserted above the line.

L. 11 (145^{3}) לגדולתו: ולגדלתו MT *et om.*

L. 12 (145^{4}) ישבחו PR Syr (?): ישבח MT *et rel.*

L. 13 (145^{5}) ידברו LXX *O′* Vulg PR: ודברי MT *et rel.*

L. 13 (145^{5}) ונפלאותיכה LXX Vulg PR: נפלאותיך MT.

L. 14 (145^{5}) אשיח: אשיחה MT.

L. 15 (145^{6}) וגדולותיכה MT ktb *Ἀ* PIH Syr (v. 6*a*): וגדולתך MT qere' Syr (v. 6*b*) *et rel.* N.B.: the third ו is inserted above the line.

L. 15 (145^{6}) אספר Syr (v. 6*a*) PIH (?): אספרנה MT LXX^{B} *Ἀ Θ Σ* (cf. *E′ ς′*): יספרו LXX Vulg PR Targ Syr (v. 6*b*).

L. 16 (145^{6-7}) Aside from orthographical considerations MT is indicated for the lacunae, except for the Q refrain.

COLUMN XVII. PS 145$^{13-21+?}$

(PL. XI)

וברוך שמו לעולם ועד 13 מלכותכה מלכות כול עולמים וממשלתכה
בכול דור ודור ברוך יהוה וברוך שמו לעולם ועד נאמן
אלוהים בדבריו וחסיד בכול מעשיו ברוך יהוה וברוך
שמו לעולם ועד 14 סומך יהוה לכול הנופלים וזוקף לכול
הכפופים ברוך יהוה וברוך שמו לעולם ועד 15 עיני
כול אליכה ישברו ואתה נותן להמה את אוכלמה בעתו
ברוך יהוה וברוך שמו לעולם ועד 16 פותח אתה את
ידכה ומשביע לכול חי רצון ברוך יהוה וברוך שמו
לעולם ועד 17 צדיק יהוה בכול דרכיו וחסיד בכול
מעשיו ברוך יהוה וברוך שמו לעולם ועד 18 קרוב יהוה
וברוך שמו לעולם ועד יקראוהו באמונה ברוך יהוה
וברוך שמו לעולם ועד 19 רצון יראיו יעשה ואת שועתמה
ישמע ויושיעם ברוך יהוה וברוך שמו לעולם ועד
20 שומר יהוה את כול יראיו ואת כול הרשעים ישמיד
ברוך יהוה וברוך שמו לעולם ועד
21 תהלת יהוה ידבר פי ויברך כול בשר את שם קודשו
ברוך יהוה וברוך שמו לעולם ו[ ] זואת לזכרון
[ ]ל̊[]ל̊[ ]ל̊[ ]ל̊[ ]

Ll. 2–3 (145$^{13 f.}$) נאמן ... מעשיו 1 ms Ken (#142) LXX Vulg PR Syr (variants: אלוהים for יהוה, and בכול[2] omitted) > MT Ά Θ Σ Έ' ς' 'Εβρ PIH Targ. (Cf. TB *Berakhot* 4*b*. Cf. *infra* v. 17*b*! The Q reading, however, is probably reliable.)

L. 6 (145^{15}) נותן N.B.: the ו is inserted above the ת.

L. 6 (145^{15}) את is inserted above the following word.

L. 7 (145^{16}) אתה LXX Vulg PR Syr > MT *et rel.*

Ll. 10–11 (145^{18}) לכל קראיו לכל אשר MT *et om.* > Q. (Cf. LXX Syr.) Scribal error ברוך — קרוב? N.B.: there should be 14 words in v. 18 with Q refrain; there are 14 words in Q v. 18. Cf. xvi 9.

L. 11 (145^{18}) באמונה : באמת MT *et al.*

L. 14 (145^{20}) יראיו Syr: אהביו MT *et rel.*

L. 16 (145^{21}) את 2 mss Ken > MT Targ. N.B.: Ken #38 and #142; cf. *supra* ll. 2–3.

L. 16 (145^{21}) לעולם ועד MT *et om.* > Q. N.B.: לעולם ועד are the last words of the Q refrain!

L. 17 (145$^{21 f.}$) זואת לזכרון > MT *et om.* A subscription on the use of the psalm (cf. Col. xxvii)? Cf. Brevard Childs's *Memory and Tradition in Israel* (1962), pp. 66 ff. N.B.: the addendum of Ken mss > Q. There is space for another composition before Ps 154.

COLUMN XVIII. (SYRIAC) PS II

(PL. XII)

לטובים נפשתכמה ולתמימים לפאר עליון [4] החבירו יחד
להודיע ישעו ואל תתעצלו להודיע עוזו ותפארתו
לכול פותאים [5] כי להודיע כבוד 𐤉𐤄𐤅𐤄 נתנה חוכמה [6] ולספר
רוב מעשיו נודעה לאדם [7] להודיע לפותאים עוזו
להשכיל לחסרי לבב גדולתו [8] הרחוקים מפתחיה
הנדחים ממבואיה [9] כי עליון הואה אדון

יעקוב ותפארתו על כול מעשיו [10] ואדם מפאר עליון
ירצה כמגיש מנחה [11] כמקריב עתודים ובני בקר
כמדשן מזבח ברוב עולות כקטורת ניחוח מיד
צדיקים [12] מפתחי צדיקים נשמע קולה ומקהל חסידים
זמרתה [13] על אוכלמה בשבע נאמרה ועל שתותמה בחבר
יחדיו [14] שיחתם בתורת עליון אמריהמה להודיע עוזו
[15] כמה רחקה מרשעים אמרה מכול זדים לדעתה [16] הנה
עיני 𐤉𐤄𐤅𐤄 על טובים תחמל [17] ועל מפאריו יגדל חסדו
מעת רעה יציל נפש[[18]] 𐤉𐤄𐤅𐤄 גואל עני מיד
זר֯[ ]ל[ ] [19]]ק֯וב֯ ו֯שופט

(Syriac) Ps No. II or Ps 154. See *infra* Part III, pp. 64–70.

COLUMN XIX. PLEA FOR DELIVERANCE

(PL. XII)

כי לוא רמה תודה לכה ולוא תספר חסדכה תולעה
חי חי יודה לכה יודו לכה כול מוטטי רגל בהודיעכה
חסדכה להמה וצדקתכה תשכילם כי בידכה נפש כול
חי נשמת כול בשר אתה נתתה עשה עמנו 𐤉𐤄𐤅𐤄
כטובכה כרוב רחמיכה וכרוב צדקותיכה שמע
𐤉𐤄𐤅𐤄 בקול אוהבי שמו ולוא עזב חסדו מהמה
ברוך 𐤉𐤄𐤅𐤄 עושה צדקות מעטר חסידיו
חסד ורחמים שאגה נפשי להלל ש[את]מכה להודות ברנה
חסדיכה להגיד אמונתכה לתהלתכה אין חקר למות
הייתי בחטאי ועוונותי לשאול מכרוני ותצילני
𐤉𐤄𐤅𐤄 כרוב רחמיכה וכרוב צדקותיכה גם אני את
שמכה אהבתי ובצלכה חסיתי בזוכרי עוזכה יתקף
לבי ועל חסדיכה אני נסמכתי סלחה 𐤉𐤄𐤅𐤄 לחטאתי
וטהרנו מעווני רוח אמונה ודעת חונני אל אתקלה
בעווה אל תשלט בי שטן ורוח טמאה מכאוב ויצר
רע אל ירשו בעצמי כי אתה 𐤉𐤄𐤅𐤄 שבחי ולכה קויתי
כול היום ישמ֯חו אחי עמי ובית אבי השוממים בחונכה
◦◦◦[ ]◦לם אשמחה בכה

Plea for Deliverance. See *infra* Part III, pp. 76–79.

COLUMN XX. PSS 139^{8-24} 137^{1}

(PL. XIII)

שאול הנכה 9אשאה כנפי שחר אשכונה באחרית ים 10שם
ידכה תנחני ותאחזני ימינכה 11ואומרה אך חושך ישופני
ולילה אזר בעדי 12גם חושך לוא יחשך ממכה ולילה
כיום יאיר כחושך כאור 13כי אתה קניתה כליותי תסוכני בבטן
אמי 14אודכה על כי נורא אתה נפלאוֹת נפלאים מעשיכה
ונפשי ידעת מואדה 15לוא נכחד עצבי ממכה אשר עשיתי̊
בסתר רוקמתי בתחתיות ארץ 16גלמי ראו עיניכה ועל
ספריכה כולם יכתבו ימים יצרו ולו באח
מהמה 17ולי מה יקרו רעיך אל על מה עצמו ראשיהם
18אספרם מחול ירבון הקיצותי ועוד עמכה 19אם
תקטול אלה רשע אנשי דמים סור מני 20אשר
יאמרוך למזמה נשאו לשוא עריך 21הלוא משנאיכה
[erasure] אשנא וממתקוממיכה אתקוטט
22תכלית שנאה שנאתים לאויבים היו לי 23חקרני
אל ודע לבי בחנני ודע סרעפי 24וראה אם דרך
עצב בי ונחני בדרך עולם
1371 על נהרות בבבל שם ישבוּ גֿ[ ] בכֿ[ ] את ציון [

L. 1 (139^{10}) גם MT LXX Lat Targ *et al.* > Q.

L. 3 (139^{11}) אזר: אור MT *et al.* (Cf. Targ קביל.) N.B.: erasure of ו after ז.

L. 3 (139^{11}) בעדי: בעדני MT *et al.*

L. 4 (139^{12}) כחושך כאור: כחשיכה כאורה MT LXX *et al.*

L. 5 (139^{14}) נורא אתה: נוראות MT *et rel.*

L. 5 (139^{14}) ? נִפְלֵאתָ LXX^{BA} Vulg PR Syr: נפליתי MT Targ *et al.* N.B.: Q probably נפלאות; final ה is lacking.

L. 6 (139^{15}) עצבי: עצמי MT *et om.*

L. 6 (139^{15}) ? עשיתו LXX Syr *et al.*: עשיתי MT Targ *et rel.* N.B.: lack of ו for *qibbuṣ*. (Cf. Introduction.)

L. 8 (139^{16}) ספריכה Syr: ספרך MT *et al.*

L. 8 (139^{16}) ולו MT qere' 2 mss Ken de Rossi: ולא MT ktb *Ά Σ Θ et rel.* ?יִלָּוֶה N.B.: poor writing surface in l. 8.

L. 8 (139^{16}) באח: אחד MT *et om.*

L. 9 (139^{16}) מהמה 3 mss (מהם) Ken de Rossi: בהם MT *et rel.*

L. 9 (139^{17}) על > MT *et rel.*

L. 9 (139^{17}) ראשיהם N.B.: the א is inserted above the ש. For רשיהם cf. *Ά Θ Ε'* PIH.

L. 10 (139^{18}) ועוד: ועודי MT *et al.*

L. 11 (139^{19}) אלה 2 mss Ken: אלוה MT *et al.*

L. 11 (139^{19}) אנשי LXX *Σ* PR PIH: ואנשי MT *et al.*

L. 11 (139^{19}) סור (cf. Syr Targ): סורו MT *et rel.*

L. 12 (139^{20}) יאמרוך MT qere' Ken de Rossi (cf. versions): יאמרך MT ktb.

L. 12 (139^{20}) נשאו (cf. versions): נָשֻׂא MT *et al. hebr.*

L. 13 (139^{21}) וממתקוממיכה: ובתקוממיך MT: ובמתקוממיך 3 mss Ken de Rossi: ומתקוממיך 2 mss Ken. N.B.: the erasures thereafter. Versions support ב.

L. 15 (139^{23}) לבי: לבבי MT *et rel. hebr.*

L. 15 (139^{23}) סרעפי Ken: שרעפי MT *et rel. hebr.*

L. 16 (139^{24}) עָצָב PIH (*idoli*) Targ (? דטעין): עֹצֶב MT *et rel.*

L. 17 (137^{1}) בבבל: בבל MT *et om.* Phonetic variant.

L. 17 (137^{1}) ישבנו N.B.: the נ is inserted above the ו.

L. 17 (137^{1}) Aside from orthographical considerations MT is indicated for the lacunae.

COLUMN XXI. PSS 137[9] 138[1–8] SIRACH 51[13 ff.]

(PL. XIII)

ונפץ את עולליך אל הסלע 138[1] לדויד אודכה
יהוה בכול לבי נגד יהוה אלוהים אזמרכה [2] אשתחוה
אל היכל קודשכה ואודה את שמכה על חסדכה ועל אמתכה
כי הגדלתה על כול שמכה אמרתכה [3] ביום קראתי ותענני
תרהיבני בנפשי עז [4] יודוך יהוה כול מלכי ארץ כי שמעו
אמרי פיכ [5] וישירו בדרכי יהוה כי גדול כבוד יהוה
[6] כי רם יהוה ושפל יראה וגבה ממרחק יידע [7] אם אלך
בתוך צרה תחיני על אף אויבי תשלח ידכה ותושיעני
ימינכה [8] יהוה יגמור בעדי יהוה חסדכה לעולם
מעשי ידיכה אל תרף
[1] אני נער בטרם תעיתי ובקשתיה [2] באה לי בתרה ועד
סופה אדורשנה [3] גם גרע נץ בבשול ענבים ישמחו לב
[4] דרכה רגלי במישור כי מנעורי ידעתיה [5] הטיתי כמעט
אוזני והרבה מצאתי לקח [6] ועלה היתה לי למלמדי אתן
הודי [7] זמותי ואשחקה קנאתי בטוב ולוא אשוב [8] חריתי
נפשי בה ופני לוא השיבותי [9] טרתי נפשי בה וברומיה לוא
אשלה [10] ידי פרש[ ]מערמיה אתבונן [11] כפי הברותי אל?
ל

L. 2 (138[1]) יהוה[1] Ken de Rossi LXX Vulg PR Targ Syr > MT PIH.

L. 2 (138[1]) יהוה[2] 1 ms Ken > MT *et rel.* N.B.: scribal error dots.

L. 5 (138[3]) עז N.B.: the peculiar shape of the ז and the erasure which follows.

L. 6 (138[4]) פיכ N.B.: the ה following the כ (medial) is erased!

L. 8 (138[7]) בקרב : בתוך MT *et rel. hebr.*

L. 8 (138[7]) ידכה MT ktb Σ Lat Syr Targ: ידיך MT qere' Ken de Rossi. Cf. LXX.

Ll. 11–18 Sirach 51[13 ff.]. See *infra* Part III, pp. 79–85.

COLUMN XXII. SIRACH 51[30] APOSTROPHE TO ZION PS 93[1-3]

(PL. XIV)

שכרכם בעתו [1]אזכירך לברכה ציון בכול מודי
אני אהבתיך ברוך לעולמים זכרך [2]גדולה תקותך ציון ושלום
ותוחלת ישועתך לבוא [3]דור ודור ידורו בך ודורות חסידים
תפארתך [4]המתאוים ליום ישעך וישישו ברוב כבודך [5]זיו
כבודך יינקו וברחובות תפארתך יעכסו [6]חסדי נביאיך
תזכורי ובמעשי חסידיך תתפארי [7]טהר חמס מגוך שקר
ועול נכרתו ממך [8]יגילו בניך בקרבך וידידיך אליך נלוו
[9]כמה קוו לישועתך ויתאבלו עליך תמיך [10]לוא תובד תקותך
ציון ולוא תשכח תוחלתך [11]מי זה אבד צדק או מי זה מלט
בעולו [12]נבחן אדם כדרכו א יש כמעשיו ישתלם [13]סביב נכרתו
צריך ציון ויתפזרו כול משנאיך [14]ערבה באף תשבחתך ציון
מעלה לכול תבל [15]פעמים רבות אזכירך לברכה בכול לבבי אברכך
[16]צדק עולמים תשיגי וברכות נכבדים תקבלי [17]קחי חזון
דובר עליך וחלמות נביאים תתבעך [18]רומי ורחבי ציון
שבחי עליון פודך תשמח נפשי בכבודך
93[1]הללויה 𐤉𐤄𐤅𐤄 מלך גאות לבש לבש 𐤉𐤄𐤅𐤄[ ]ויתאזר אף
[ ]כׄןׄ תבל בל טמוט [2]נכון כסאכה מאׄזׄ מׄ[ ]לׄםׄ [ ][3]נשׄאׄו נהרות

L. 1 Sirach 51[30b]. See *infra* Part III, pp. 79–85.

Ll. 1–15 Apostrophe to Zion. See *infra* Part III, pp. 85–89.

L. 16 (93[1]) הללויה > MT *et om.*

L. 16 (93[1]) ויתאזר LXX (*καὶ περιεζώσατο*) Lat Targ Syr: התאזר MT *et rel. hebr.*

L. 17 (93[1]) תכֵן 1 ms Ken LXX (*ἐστερέωσεν*) Vulg PR (PIH?) Syr Targ: תכון MT *et rel. hebr.*

L. 17 (93[1]) טמוט: תמוט MT *et om.*

Ll. 16–17 (93[1–3]) Aside from orthographical considerations MT is indicated for the lacunae. N.B.: the strange configurations (with ה?) in a different hand (?) in the left margin. Ps 141 would have followed directly.

COLUMN XXIII. PSS 141^{5-10} 133^{1-3} 144^{1-7}

(PL. XIV)

ויוכיחני שמן רואש אל יני רואשי כי עוד וׄתלפתׄי
ברעותיהמה 6 נשמטו בידי סלע שופטיהם וׄשמעו
אמרי כי נע מו 7 כמו פלח וׄבקע בארץ נפזרו עצמי לפי
אשאול 8 כי אליכה 𐤉𐤄𐤅𐤄 אדוני עיני בכה חסיתי אל
תער נפשי 9 שמורני מיד פח יקושו לי ומוקשות פועלי און
10 יפולו במכמריו רשעים יחד אנוכי עד אעבוׄר
133 1 שיר ה מעלות לדויד הנה מה טוב ומה
נעים שבת אחים גם יחד 2 כשמן הטוב על הרואש
יורד על הזקן זקן אהרון שירד על פי מדיו 3 כטל חרמון
שיורד על הר ציון כי שמה צוה 𐤉𐤄𐤅𐤄 את הברכה עד
עולם שלום על ישראל
144 1 ברוך 𐤉𐤄𐤅𐤄 צורי המלמׄד ידי לקרב ואצבעותי למלחמה
2 חסדי ומצודתי משגבי ומפלט לי מגני ובו חסיתי הרודד
עמים תחתי 3 אלוהים מה אדם ותדעהו בן אנוש
ותחושבהו 4 אדם להבל דמה וימיו כצל עובר 5 אלוהים הט
שמיכה ורד גע בה[ ]ויעשנו 6 ברק ברק ותפיצם שלחׄ חצ°°°
[? 7]כה ממרום פצני והציל[ ]

L. 1 (141^{5}) ותלפתי: ותפלתי MT *et om.* (metathesis?). Possibly יתלפתו.

L. 3 (141^{6}) נעמו N.B.: erasure of י (?) after ע.

L. 3 (141^{7}) עצמי: עצמינו MT *et al.* (Gunkel emended MT to עצמי on the basis of Ps Sol 16^{1-2}.)

L. 5 (141^{9}) מיד (Syr): מידי MT *et al. hebr.* PIH Targ.

L. 5 (141^{9}) יקושו: יקשו MT. Cf. Introduction.

L. 6 (141^{10}) אעבור N.B.: the ו is inserted above the ר.

L. 9 (133^{2}) מדיו: מדותיו MT *et rel. hebr.*

L. 10 (133^{3}) הר 1 ms Ken PR Syr: הררי MT *et rel.*

L. 10 (133^{3}) שמה (cf. Gunkel): שם MT *et rel. hebr.*

L. 10 (133^{3}) חיים MT *et om.* > Q. (Cf. Baethgen, Buhl, *et al.*)

L. 11 (133^{3}) עולם 3 mss Ken (cf. Budde): העולם MT *et rel. hebr.*

L. 11 ($133^{3\,f.}$) שלום על ישראל (cf. iv 8 and MT Ps 128^{6}) > MT *et rel.* Cf. Ken on Ps 122^{9}.

L. 12 (144^{1}) לדוד MT *et al.* > Q 4 mss Ken.

L. 12 (144^{1}) המלמד N.B.: the second מ is inserted above the ד.

L. 12 (144^{1}) ואצבעותי Ken OL Vulg mss PR Syr: אצבעותי MT LXX PIH Targ.

L. 13 (144^{2}) ומפלט: ומפלטי MT *et al.*

L. 14 (144^{2}) עמים (cf. Ps 18^{48} II Sam 22^{48}) MT^{sebir} Ken de Rossi *A* PR PIH Targ Syr: עמי MT LXX^{B} Vulg.

L. 14 (144^{3}) אלוהים: יהוה MT *et om.* (Cf. *infra* l. 15.)

L. 14 (144^{3}) N.B.: poor writing surface and erasure (of ות?) at end of line.

L. 15 (144^{4}) וימיו Syr: ימיו MT *et rel.*

L. 15 (144^{5}) אלוהים: יהוה MT *et om.* (Cf. *supra* l. 14.)

L. 16 (144^{5}) ורד LXX Vulg PR: ותרד MT *et rel.*

L. 16 (144^{5}) בהרים of MT indicated for lacuna.

L. 16 (144^{6}) N.B.: poor writing surface and/or erasure at end of line.

L. 17 (144^{6-7}) Aside from orthographical considerations MT is indicated for the lacunae. N.B.: space avoided at the beginning of the line?

COLUMN XXIV. PS 144[15] (SYRIAC) PS III

(PL. XV)

15 אשרי העם שככה לו אשרי העם אשר 𐤉𐤄𐤅𐤄 𐤉𐤄𐤅𐤄
אלוהיו
1 𐤉𐤄𐤅𐤄 קראתי אליכה הקשיבה אלי 2 פרשתי כפי
למעון קודשכה 3 הט אוזנכה ותן לי את שאלתי 4 ובקשתי
אל תמנע ממני 5 בנה נפשי ואל תמגרה 6 ואל תפרע לפני
רשעים 7 גמולי הרע ישיב ממני דין האמת 8 𐤉𐤄𐤅𐤄 𐤉𐤄𐤅𐤄
אל תשפטני כחטאתי כי לוא יצדק לפניכה כול חי
9 הבינני 𐤉𐤄𐤅𐤄 בתורתכה ואת משפטיכה למדני
10 וישמעו רבים מעשיכה ועמים יהדרו את כבודכה
11 זכורני ואל תשכחני ואל תביאני בקשות ממני
12 חטאת נעורי הרחק ממני ופשעי אל יזכרו לי
13 טהרני 𐤉𐤄𐤅𐤄 מנגע רע ואל יוסף לשוב אלי 14 יבש
שׁרשיו ממני ואל ינצו ע[ ]יו בי 15 כבוד אתה 𐤉𐤄𐤅𐤄
על כן שאלתי מלפניכה שלמה 16 למי אזעקה ויתן לי
ובני אדם מה יוסיף אומ[ ] 17 מׄלפׄ[ ]יכה 𐤉𐤄𐤅𐤄 מבטחי
קראתי 𐤉𐤄𐤅𐤄 ויענני [ ]שבר לבי 18 נמתי
[ ]שנה חלמתי גם [𐤉𐤄𐤅[𐤄

L. 1 (144[15]) אשר יהוה: שיהוה MT *et rel. hebr.* Ll. 3–17 (Syriac) Ps No. III or Ps 155. See *infra* Part III, pp. 70–76. Ps 142 would have followed directly.

COLUMN XXV. PSS 142^{4-8} 143^{1-8}

(PL. XV)

לי 5אביטה ימין וראה ואין לי מכיר אבד מנוס ממני אין
דורש לנפשי 6זעקתי אליכה 𐤉𐤄𐤅𐤄 אמרתי אתה מחסי
חלקי בארץ החיים 7הקשיבה אל רנתי כי דלותי מואדה
הצילני מרודפי כי אמצו ממני 8הוצא ממסגר נפשי להודות
את שמכה בי יכת רו צדיקים כי תגמול עלי
143 1מזמור לדויד 𐤉𐤄𐤅𐤄 שמעה תפלתי
האזינה אל תחנוני באמונתכה ענני בצדקתכה 2ואל
תבוא במשפט את עבדכה כי לוא יצדק לפניכה כול חי 3כי
ירדוף אויב נפשי דכ֯א לארץ חיתי הושיבני במחשכים
כמיתי עולם 4ותתעטף עלי רוחי בתוכי וישתומם לבבי
5זכרתי ימים מקדם הגיתי בו֯ל פועלכה במעשי ידיכה
אשיחה 6פרשתי ידי א[ ]ה֯ נפשי בארץ עיפה לכה סלה
7מהר ענני 𐤉𐤄𐤅𐤄 כ֯[ ]רוחי אל תסתר פניכה ממני
ונמשלתי עם יור[8]ש[ ]י בבוקר חסדכה
[ ]???[אליכה נשא[ ]

L. 1 (142^{5}) אביטה ימין וראה LXX (*κατενόουν εἰς τὰ δεξιὰ καὶ ἐπέβλεπον*) Vulg PR (*considerabam ad dexteram et videbam*) Targ Syr: הביט ימין וראה MT PIH.

L. 5 (142^{8}) יכתרו N.B.: erasure of י after the ת; Q = MT. For hif'il cf. Ken.

L. 5 (142^{8}) צדיקים N.B.: erasure (?) before the צ.

L. 9 (143^{3}) ירדוף: רדף MT *et om.*

L. 9 (143^{3}) דכא N.B.: the א is inserted above the erasure of a ה (?). For דכה cf. Ken.

L. 10 (143^{4}) וישתומם Syr PR: ישתומם MT *et rel.*

L. 10 (143^{4}) לבבי 1 ms Ken (#219): לבי MT.

L. 11 (143^{5}) בכול N.B.: the כ is inserted above the ו.

L. 11 (143^{5}) במעשי Ken de Rossi LXX Σ Lat Targ: במעשה MT Syr *et al.*

L. 12 (143^{5}) אשיחה: אשוחח MT *et rel. hebr.* (Cf. Ps 145^{5}; 119 *passim*; cf. xvi 14.)

L. 12 (143^{6}) בארץ Ken: כארץ MT *et rel.*

L. 12 (143^{6}) עיפה N.B.: the י is inserted above the פ; erasure of a י (?) preceding the ע. Q = MT.

Ll. 12–15 (143^{6-8}) Aside from orthographical considerations MT is indicated for the lacunae and Ps 149 would have followed directly. The traces before אליכה come from Col. xxvi?

COLUMN XXVI. PSS 149^{7-9} 150^{1-6} HYMN TO THE CREATOR

(PL. XVI)

7לעשות נקמה בגויים תוכחות בלאומים 8לאסור מלכיהם
בזקים ונכבדיהםה בכבלי ברזל 9לעשות בהם משפט כתוב
הדר הוא לכול חסידיו לבני ישראל עם קודשו הללו יה
150 1הללו אל בקודשו הללוהו ברקיע עוזו 2הללוהו
בגבורותיו הללוהו כרוב גודלו 3הללוהו בתקוע שופר הללוהו
בנבל וכנור 4הללוהו בתוף ומחול הללוהו במנים ועוגב
5הללוהו בצלצלי שמע הללוהו בצלצלי תרועה 6כול הנשמות
תהלליה הללויה
1גדול וקדוש 𐤉𐤄𐤅𐤄 קדוש קדושים לדור ודור 2לפניו הדר
ילך ואחריו המון מים רבים 3חסד ואמת סביב פניו אמת
ומשפט וצדק מכון כסאו 4מבדיל אור מאפלה שחר הכין בדעת
לבו 5אזראו כול מלאכיו וירננו כי הראם את אשר לוא ידעו
6מעטר הרים תנובות אוכל טוב לכול חי 7ברוך עושה
ארץ בכוחו מכין תבל בחוכמתו 8בתבונתו נטה שמים ויוצא
[ ] מאו[9]ר֯ עשה ויעל נ֯שיא֯[ ]ק֯צ֯ה

L. 3 (149^{9}) לבני ישראל עם קודשו : לבני ישראל עם קרובו 1 ms Ken (#40) > MT *et rel.* Cf. Ps 148^{14}.
L. 4 (150^{1}) הללו יה MT *et rel. hebr.* PIH Targ > Q 3 mss Ken Syr. Haplography? Cf. LXX PR.
L. 5 (150^{3}) בתקוע : בתקע MT *et al. hebr.*
L. 7 (150^{6}) הנשמות : הנשמה MT *et om.*
Ll. 9 ff. Hymn to the Creator. See *infra* Part III, pp. 89–91.

COLUMN XXVII. II SAM 23^{7} DAVID'S COMPOSITIONS PS 140$^{1-5}$

(PL. XVI)

ועץ חי̊צני̊ת ובאש שרף ישרפו בשבת
ויהי דויד בן ישי חכם ואור כאור השמש ס̊ופר
ונבון ותמים בכול דרכיו לפני אל ואנשים ויתן
לו 𐤉𐤄𐤅𐤄 רוח נבונה ואורה ויכתוב תהלים
שלושת אלפים ושש מאות ושיר לשורר לפני המזבח על עולת
התמיד לכול יום ויום לכול ימי השנה ארבעה וששים ושלוש
מאות ולקורבן השבתות שנים וחמשים שיר ולקורבן ראשי
החודשים ולכול ימי המועדות ולי ם הכפורים שלושים שיר
ויהי כול השיר אשר דבר ששה ואבעים וארבע מאות ושיר
לנגן על הפגו̊עים ארבעה ויהי הכול ארבעת אלפים וחמשים
כול אלה דבר בנבואה אשר נתן לו מלפני העליון
140^{1} למנצח מזמור לדויד ^{2}חלצני 𐤉𐤄𐤅𐤄
מאדם רע מ[]יש חמסים תצרני ^{3}אשר חשבו רעות בלב כול
היום יגרו̊ [ ]ל[]מות ^{4}שננו לשונם כמו נחש חמת עכביש תחת
[ ]^{5}שו̊מרני 𐤉𐤄𐤅𐤄 מידי ר̊שע̊ מאיש[ ]

L. 1 (II Sam 23^{7}) חיצנית ?: חנית MT *et om.* Read חצינות ? Cf. Ps 57^{5} חנית וחצים.

L. 1 (II Sam 23^{7}) שרף N.B.: erasures indicate an original שרוף with scribal dots over the last two letters.

Ll. 2–11. David's Compositions. See *infra* Part III, pp. 91–93.

L. 13 (Ps 140^{2}) חמסים N.B.: the ס is written over a י.

L. 13 (140^{2}) תצרני 3 mss Ken: תנצרני MT *et rel. hebr.*

L. 14 (140^{3}) היום 5 mss Ken Grk *et al.*: יום MT *et rel.*

L. 14 (140^{3}) יגרו Targ Syr: יגורו MT *et rel.* (Cf. Olshausen, Gunkel, *et al.* יָגֹרוּ.)

L. 14 (140^{4}) עכביש (cf. Isa 59^{5}) Targ (עכוביתא): עכשוב MT *et rel.*

Ll. 13–15 (140$^{2-5}$) Aside from orthographical considerations MT is indicated for the lacunae and Ps 134 would have followed directly.

COLUMN XXVIII. PSS 134$^{1-3}$ 151 A AND B

(PL. XVII)

𐤉𐤄𐤅𐤄 העומדים בבית 𐤉𐤄𐤅𐤄 בלילות 2 שאו ידיכם קודש וברכו
את שם 𐤉𐤄𐤅𐤄 3 יברככה 𐤉𐤄𐤅𐤄 מציו[] עושה שמים וארץ

151 A הללויה לדויד בן ישי 1 קטן הייתי מ⸢ו⸣אחי וצעיר מבני אבי וישימני
רועה לצונו ומושל בגדיותיו 2 ידי עשו עוגב ואצבעותי כנור
ואשימה ל𐤉𐤄𐤅𐤄 כבוד אמרתי אני בנפשי 3 ההרים לוא יעידו
לו והגבעות לוא יגידו עלו֯ העצים את דברי֯ והצואן את מעשי֯
4 כי מי יגיד ומי ידבר ומי יספר את מעשי֯ אדון הכול ראה אלוה
הכול הוא שמע והוא האזין 5 שלח נביאו למושחני את שמואל
לגדלני יצאו אחי לקראתו יפי התור ויפי המראה 6 הגבהים בקומתם
היפים בשערם לוא בחר 𐤉𐤄𐤅𐤄 אלוהים בם 7 וישלח ויקחני
מאחר הצואן וימשחני בשמן הקודש וישימני נגיד לעמו ⸢ומושל⸣ בבני
בריתו
151 B תחלת גב[]רה ל[ ]יד משמשחו נביא אלוהים 1 אזי רא֯[]תי פלשתי
מחרף ממ֯[ ]אנוכי[ ]את[ ]

L. 1 (134[2]) ידיכם MT qere' Ken: ידכם MT ktb.
L. 2 (134[2]) שם > MT *et om.*
L. 2 (134[3]) מציון N.B.: the ן is obliterated by a tear in the skin surface.

Ll. 3–12. Ps 151 A. See *infra* Part III, pp. 54–64.
Ll. 13–14. The beginning of Ps 151 B. See *infra* Part III, pp. 60–64.

III

The Apocryphal Compositions

NOS. I, II, AND III OF THE FIVE SYRIAC APOCRYPHAL PSALMS*

IN Cols. xviii, xxiv, and xxviii are found, save for a few lines of text missing at the bottoms of Cols. xvii, xviii, xxiv, and xxviii, Hebrew texts of Pss I (LXX Ps 151), II, and III of the five Syriac non-canonical psalms which appear as 'filler' material in a Book of Discipline (*kᵉṯâḇâ ḏᵉ-ḏūrâšâ*) by the tenth-century Nestorian Bishop Elijah of al-Anbar.[(1)]

The Assemani, in 1759, were the first to note the existence of the Syriac psalms in a manuscript in the Vatican.[(2)] In 1887 W. Wright published a text of the five psalms from a manuscript in the University Library of Cambridge.[(3)] In 1899 E. Sachau noted the existence of the same psalms in a manuscript in Berlin.[(4)] In 1927 A. Mingana published the texts of the psalms from two manuscripts in the Rendel Harris Library, Selly Oak, Birmingham, England, Ming 31 dated to *ca.* 1340, and Ming 51 dated to *ca.* 1550.[(5)]

In 1930 Professor Martin Noth, principally using Ming 31, published a collated text with German translation of the five psalms.[(6)] He also translated the Syriac back into Hebrew of three of the five, Nos. II, III, and IV.

Unavailable to Professor Noth at the time were three as-yet-unpublished manuscripts of the five psalms. Two of these afford the only biblical manuscripts in which the group of psalms occurs: a Nestorian twelfth-century manuscript of the Psalter (Mosul/Baghdad, Library of the Chaldean Patriarchate 1113), and a Nestorian text of the prophets dated A.D. 1813 (Berlin, German State Library 3122); the third is yet another copy of the Bishop's handbook dated A.D. 1863 (Woodbrooke, Selly Oak College Library, Ming Syr 579). The latter two are rigidly faithful to the Syriac tradition represented in Ming 31. By contrast, the Mosul text offers significant variants in Pss II and III (numbered in the manuscript as Pss 154 and 155!), as well as interesting marginal notes, and provides the most faithful Syriac version of the psalms available to date.

In 1958 and 1959 respectively M. Delcor and M. Philonenko both suggested that the five psalms were essentially Essenian.[(7)]

The reader would be well advised to consult the Syriac texts as they are presented in Professor Noth's article in *Zeitschrift für die alttestamentliche Wissenschaft*, xlviii (1930), pp. 5–7. The Hebrew texts are here presented in metrical arrangement, and the reading notes are offered according to the resultant versification. For convenience of reference to the Syriac text, as well as to Noth's Hebrew translation of the Syriac, the corresponding line numbers of the Syriac are given with the verse references to the Hebrew.

* The material in this section has appeared in another form in the *Zeitschrift für die alttestamentliche Wissenschaft*, lxxv (1963), pp. 73–86, and lxxvi (1964), pp. 57–75.

(1) One-third of the width of 11QPsᵃ was destroyed by dampness in the cave in antiquity. Cf. *Bulletin of the American Schools of Oriental Research*, clxv (1962), pp. 11–15, and *supra* pp. 3–5.

(2) *Bibliothecae Apostolicae Vaticanae Codicum manuscriptorum Catalogus*, Partis Primae, Tomus Tertius (1759), pp. 385–6.

(3) *Proceedings of the Society of Biblical Archaeology*, ix (1887), pp. 257 ff.

(4) Sachau, *Verzeichniss der syrischen Handschriften der königlichen Bibliothek zu Berlin*, i (1899), p. 209.

(5) *Bulletin of the John Rylands Library*, xi (1927), pp. 492–8, reprinted in *Woodbrooke Studies*, i (1927), pp. 288–94.

(6) 'Die fünf syrisch überlieferten apokryphen Psalmen', *Zeitschrift für die alttestamentliche Wissenschaft*, xlviii (1930), pp. 1–23. Cf. now *List of Old Testament Peshitta Manuscripts*, Peshitta Institute, Leiden, 1961, p. 113.

(7) Delcor, 'Cinq nouveaux psaumes esséniens?', *Revue de Qumrân*, i (1958), pp. 85–102. Philonenko, 'L'Origine essénienne des cinq psaumes syriaques de David', *Semitica*, ix (1959), pp. 35–48. These articles are hereafter referred to by the names of the authors. See now M. Delcor, *Les Hymnes de Qumrân* (1962), pp. 299–319.

PS 151 A, B—(SYRIAC) PSALM I (11QPs^a 151)

Col. XXVIII ll. 3–14

While LXX Ps 151 is also known as Ps 151 in the Syro-Hexaplar,(1) in the group of five Syriac apocryphal psalms it is No. I, so called since Wright first published them in 1887.

In 1908 Spoer published the text of a Syriac manuscript of Ps 151, which he had located in the Syrian Convent in Jerusalem and which dates from A.D. 1472.(2) His text, the Syro-Hexaplar Codex Ambrosianus, the LXX, and OL(3) lack, before v. 2, a verse which is common to the Syriac manuscripts (except Mosul) which contain the five psalms: 'And I found a lion and a wolf [bear?] and slew them and rent them.' It has been the consensus that the verse is an interpolation from Syriac Pss IV and V, which purport to have been written by David on the occasion of his having smitten the wild beasts as a shepherd protecting his father's flocks (I Sam 17$^{34-37}$). That the Qumrân and Mosul texts also fail to mention the lion–bear episode confirms the consensus. It is further the consensus that without the lion–bear verse, then, Syriac Ps I, in all the manuscripts, is clearly a translation of LXX Ps 151.

11QPs 151 A comprises seven verses of two lines each, each line being a distich. There are fourteen distichs, ten of which are 3/2 and four of which are 3/3. The four hexameters are in vv. 4 and 7, each of which marks the end of a strophe, or sense division, of the psalm.

Nine of the fourteen lines or distichs have synonymous parallelism, or as closely synonymous as the Qinah metre permits. Four have synthetic parallelism (vv. *2b*, *5b*, *6b*, *7a*) and one has the 'stairlike' structure (*4a*).

The poem easily divides itself into two strophes, both by metre and by content. The first strophe deals with David's musical ability and his praise of God thereby. The second strophe deals with God's sending the prophet Samuel to anoint David instead of his brothers.

The Hebrew psalm supports more than one translation. The rendering here offered has already provoked several alternative, very welcome suggestions.(4)

The following is a line-by-line comparison of 11QPs 151 A (xxviii 3–12) and LXX Ps 151$^{1-5}$, with a translation of the Hebrew and notes to the text. Distinctive elements in each are underscored.

PSALM 151 A

LXX	Q
Οὗτος ὁ ψαλμὸς ἰδιόγραφος εἰς Δαυεὶδ καὶ ἔξωθεν τοῦ ἀριθμοῦ, ὅτε ἐμονομάχησεν τῷ Γολιάδ.	הללויה לדויד בן ישי

(1) Codex Ambrosianus. Cf. A. M. Ceriani, *Monumenta Sacra et Profana*, vii, Milan, 1874. Cf. H. Schneider, 'Biblische Oden im syrohexaplarischen Psalter', *Biblica*, xl (1959), pp. 202–5.

(2) *Zeitschrift für die alttestamentliche Wissenschaft*, xxviii (1908), pp. 65–67.

(3) Cf. 'Liber Psalmorum' of the *Biblia Sacra*, Rome, 1953, *ad loc*. Cf. also Pierre Salmon's *Les 'Tituli Psalmorum' des manuscrits latins*, Rome, (1960), series 1 and 2, *ad loc*.

(4) The *editio princeps* of 11QPs 151 appeared in the *Zeitschrift für die alttestamentliche Wissenschaft*, lxxv (1963), pp. 73–85. The following treatment of Ps 151 A is basically the same as appeared earlier but with several corrections and adjustments. I am aware of four articles which will have appeared before publication of this volume: Patrick Wm. Skehan, 'The Apocryphal Psalm 151', *The Catholic Biblical Quarterly*, xxv (1963), pp. 407–9; J. Carmignac, 'La Forme poétique du Psaume 151 de la grotte 11', *Revue de Qumrân*, iv (1963), pp. 371–8; W. H. Brownlee, 'The 11Q Counterpart to Psalm 151, 1–5', *Revue de Qumrân*, iv (1963), pp. 379–87; and I. Rabinowitz, 'The Alleged Orphism of 11QPss 28, 3–12', *Zeitschrift für die alttestamentliche Wissenschaft*, lxxvi (1964), pp. 193–200. Professor W. F. Albright by correspondence has proposed a seventh–sixth-century B.C. date for Ps 151; cf. his *History, Archaeology and Christian Humanism* (1964), p. 35. I am grateful to all these scholars for sharing their work in advance of publication. However, there is such wide divergence of opinion that, as F. M. Cross has privately suggested, there may well be no early agreement: e.g., ll. 5–7 may be read in at least three distinct senses (see especially Rabinowitz and Skehan).

Greek	Hebrew	Col. XXVIII Lines
151¹ *Μικρὸς ἤμην ἐν τοῖς ἀδελφοῖς μου,* *καὶ νεώτερος ἐν τῷ οἴκῳ τοῦ πατρός μου·* *ἐποίμαινον τὰ πρόβατα τοῦ πατρός μου.*	קטן הייתי מן אחי וצעיר מבני אבי וישימני רועה לצונו ומושל בגדיותיו	(1) 3–4
² *αἱ χεῖρές μου ἐποίησαν ὄργανον,* *οἱ δάκτυλοί μου ἥρμοσαν ψαλτήριον.*	ידי עשו עוגב ואצבעותי כנור ואשימה ליהוה כבוד אמרתי אני בנפשי	(2) 4–5
Lacking	ההרים לוא יעידו לו והגבעות לוא יגידו עלו העצים את דברי והצואן את מעשי	(3) 5–6
³ *καὶ τίς ἀναγγελεῖ τῷ κυρίῳ μου* *αὐτὸς κύριος, αὐτὸς εἰσακούει.*	כי מי יגיד ומי ידבר ומי יספר את מעשי אדון הכול ראה אלוה הכול הוא שמע והוא האזין	(4) 7–8
⁴ᵃ *αὐτὸς ἐξαπέστειλεν τὸν ἄγγελον αὐτοῦ* ⁵ᵃ *οἱ ἀδελφοί μου καλοὶ καὶ μεγάλοι*	שלח נביאו למושחני את שמואל לגדלני יצאו אחי לקראתו יפי התור ויפי המראה	(5) 8–9
⁵ᵇ *καὶ οὐκ εὐδόκησεν κύριος ἐν αὐτοῖς*	הגבהים בקומתם היפים בשערם לוא בחר יהוה אלוהים בם	(6) 9–10
⁴ᵇ *καὶ ἦρέν με ἐκ τῶν προβάτων τοῦ πατρός μου,* ⁴ᶜ *καὶ ἔχρισέν με ἐν τῷ ἐλαίῳ τῆς χρίσεως αὐτοῦ.*	וישלח ויקחני מאחר הצואן וימשחני בשמן הקודש וישימני נגיד לעמו ומושל בבני בריתו	(7) 10–12

A Hallelujah of David the Son of Jesse.

1. Smaller was I than my brothers
   and the youngest of the sons of my father,
   So he made me shepherd of his flock
   and ruler over his kids.

2. My hands have made an instrument
   and my fingers a lyre;
   And [so] have I rendered glory to the Lord,
   thought I, within my soul.

3. The mountains do not witness to him,
   nor do the hills proclaim;
   The trees have cherished my words
   and the flock my works.

4. For who can proclaim and who can bespeak
   and who can recount the deeds of the Lord?
   Everything has God seen,
   everything has he heard and he has heeded.

5. He sent his prophet to anoint me,
   Samuel to make me great;
   My brothers went out to meet him,
   handsome of figure and appearance.

6. Though they were tall of stature
   and handsome by their hair,
   The Lord God chose
   them not.

7. But he sent and took me from behind the flock
   and anointed me with holy oil,
   And he made me leader of his people
   and ruler over the sons of his covenant.

The poem is a poetic midrash on I Sam 16^{1-13}, the attractively simple account of how the shepherd David, Jesse's eighth and youngest son, was made ruler of Israel. Just as in I Kings 3^{5-15} Solomon protested his youth (אנכי נער קטן), so David here begins by noting his. But the point of David's election in the Bible is the crux of the poetic midrash: 'The Lord looks upon the heart' (I Sam 16^{7}). However, the biblical passage fails to state what God saw in David's heart, and it is just that which the poetic midrash supplies. Even though David is insignificant in external appearance, he, in his soul or heart or to himself, has said the significant thing: he would give glory to the Lord (v. 2); and the Lord, who can see into the heart, has seen and heard everything David has done and said (v. 4). Therefore God heeded David's piety of soul by sending the prophet Samuel to take him from behind the flock to make him a great ruler.

The first strophe (vv. 1–4) deals with David and what he thought and did to praise God, and how God, who sees into the heart, heeded David's soul-prayer. What David thought and did, his 'words' and 'works' (v. 3*b*), are represented by the scroll itself and the '4,050 psalms and songs' of Col. xxvii 2–11. The second strophe (vv. 5–7) deals with God's response, through Samuel, to David's desire by making David great, where he had been insignificant (vv. 1 and 5), and by anointing him ruler of his people, where he had been only a ruler of flocks (vv. 1*b* and 7*b*).

V. 1*a* (l. 3):
קטן. Cf. I Sam 16^{11} and 17^{14} of David and I Kings 3^{7} of Solomon.
צעיר. Cf. Ps 119^{141} (xii 14) צעיר אנכי ונבזה; Judg 6^{15} ואנכי הצעיר בבית אבי; and Micah 5^{1} of Bethlehem.
מבני. LXX and Syr בבית?

V. 1*b* (l. 4):
רועה. Cf. I Sam 16^{11} עוד שאר הקטן והנה רעה בצאן.
מושל. Cf. Ps 105^{21}.

V. 2*a* (l. 4):
עוגב, כנור. Cf. Gen 4^{21} Job 30^{31}.

V. 2*b* (l. 5):
ואשימה. Cf. Isa 42^{12} ישימו ליהוה כבוד, 'Let them render glory to the Lord'. The conflate *he* may be artificial as in two-thirds of its occurrences in the scroll (see Introduction); or it may be cohortative and the *waw* conjunctive. The syntax is not necessarily classical and the *waw* is not of necessity consecutive; and it may mean 'then' or 'so' as frequently in Qohelet.

אמרתי. 'To think' or 'to intend' as in Ex 2^{14}.

בנפשי. Cf. Qoh $2^{1, 15}$ $3^{17, 18}$ אמרתי אני בלבי. Both בלבי and בנפשי mean 'to myself': but the poet here chose the latter. נפש for him may have had some of the same significance it must have had for Josephus (*Antiquities*, vi. 160, on I Sam 16^{7}, quoted below).

The phrase אמרתי אני בלבי usually precedes the thought expressed. It is possible, of course, that the phrase here should introduce v. 3, but not probable in the context. The poem tells what wonderful thing it was which God saw in David's heart, that which inclined him to choose David over his handsome brothers: clearly it was David's soul-prayer that his music should have rendered glory to God.

V. 3*a* (ll. 5–6):
Cf. Micah 6^{1-2}, where mountains and hills amply witness God's judgements in the covenant lawsuit, or Isa 44^{23} and 55^{12}, where nature responds in joy to God's work of salvation. To say that mountains and hills do not witness to God or proclaim his deeds (cf. v. 4*a*) is non-biblical.

V. 3*b* (l. 6):
עָלוֹ. Cf. Jastrow, p. 1081, and CD iii 2 and v 5. As noted above in v. 2, the Hebrew of the poem is not necessarily classical; on the contrary it is an archaizing use of classical Hebrew in the post-biblical period. Attempts to read לוֹ//עָלוֹ [and דברו, מעשו?] or עֲלֵי leave v. 3*b* without a verb. Does not v. 3 say in beauty and simplicity that mute nature appreciates David's masterful music in praise of God? One would, of course, prefer that a *waw* had been prefixed to עלו, and perhaps it was lost by haplography.

V. 4*a* (ll. 7–8):
כי מי יגיד. Cf. Isa 40^{12-13} Sirach 16^{26} 17^{17} 39^{16-17} 42^{17} 43^{30-32}. No one can fully recount God's deeds (despite Ps 118^{17} ואספר מעשי יה).

אדון. Cf. Ps 114^{7}, God (French *Maître*). The biblical phrase is האדון יהוה, especially in Isaiah. אדון is construct only to כל הארץ in the Bible, never to הכול (nor in Qumrân literature). Note that the phrase, in reference to God in Ps 114^{7}, is interesting also in that the context of the psalm is that of mountains, hills, and flocks (called to my attention by J. Carmignac). Cf. 1QH x 8 אדון לכול רוח, and Skehan's article cited in note 4, p. 54.

V. 4*b* (l. 8):
הכול ראה. Cf. I Sam 30^{19} הכל השיב דוד; II Chron 36^{17} הכל נתן בידו; Qoh 7^{15} את הכל ראיתי. Also note the usage in 1QH xvi 8 אשר מעשיך הכול. The point the poet makes here is the point already made in I Sam 16^{7} that God sees absolutely everything, not just externals but even and especially what is going on in David's heart (or soul!): ויהוה יראה ללבב. Cf. I Sam 13^{14} בקש יהוה לו איש and Ps 78^{72} וירעם כתם לבבו, of David.

אלוה. Absolute usage as for אדון. The occurrence in Ps 114^{7} (*sic*) is the only instance of the construct I have found in the Bible, or Qumrân. Note erasure of prefixed *waw* with scribal dot over it (see 'Surface Observations' in Part I), which indicates the scribe, on reflection, took אלוה as absolute.

שמע . . . האזין. God has heard David's music and heeded what is in his heart (and/or soul, I Sam 16^{7} Ps 78^{72}), his great desire to give God glory (v. 2*b*) even though God is above all praise (vv. 3–4). David's music, of course, would be well represented by the scroll in hand! N.B.: LXX$^{\aleph}$ *et al.* read αὐτὸς πάντων εἰσακούει (= הכול הוא שמע).

V. 5 (ll. 8–9):
A poetic recapitulation of the story in I Sam $16^{4 ff.}$.

יפי. Cf. Gen 29^{17} 39^{6} ויהי יוסף יפה תאר ויפה מראה.

התור (התואר). Cf. I Chron 17^{17} (כתור—LXX ὡς ὅρασις), 1QIs^{b} 52^{14} (ותרו—MT ותארו), 11QPs^{a} xxi 11 (בתרה); and *supra* v. 1*bβ*.

V. 6 (ll. 9–10):

קומתם. Cf. I Sam 16^{7} of Eliab, אל תבט אל מראהו ואל גבה קומתו.

לוא בחר. Cf. I Sam 16^{8-10} לא בחר יהוה באלה. If the same poetic metre is maintained here as in the rest of the poem then the proper emphasis is conveyed from the biblical text to the poem. A rallentando stress on each syllable emphasizes the climax of the poem.

V. 7 (ll. 10–12):

מאחר הצואן. Cf. Ps 78^{70-71} II Sam 7^{8} (Amos 7^{15}).
שמן הקודש. Cf. Ps 89^{21}. Cf. LXX Syr.

V. *7b* (ll. 11–12):

Note the parallel correspondence with v. *1b*. Cf. Ps 78^{72} וירעם כתם לבבו.
נגיד לעמו. Usually נגיד על עמו.
בני בריתו. Cf. 1QM xvii 8 and cf. ישראל in Micah 5^{1} and II Chron 7^{18}.

The superscriptions in LXX and Old Latin in no way compare with the superscription in Q or in the Syriac. The latter reads 'A Todah [or Hodayah] of David', and Q reads 'A Hallelujah of David the son of Jesse'. Only in the superscription is the Syriac closer to Q than to LXX. 'Hallelujah' in Q is a title or type of psalm as in Pss 146–50.[1] The phrase 'the son of Jesse' is unique in psalter superscriptions and has as companion only the subscription to Ps 72.

The three major points of the LXX superscription (retained verbatim in Old Latin) are significantly lacking in Q. The protest evident in ἰδιόγραφος suggests, perhaps, a doubt about authorship which the faithful at Qumrân did not entertain. On the contrary, in the Qumrân psalter this psalm occurs in the last column in such a position as to suggest that it held great importance in Qumrânian beliefs concerning both David and his musical ability. Nothing in 11QPs[a] contradicts this; on the contrary, the last two columns of the scroll confirm it. For, in the preceding Col. xxvii, are 'the last words of David' of II Sam 23^{7} and a prose composition listing all the types of musical compositions David wrote, giving a precise number for each genre and then giving the sum as 4,050. The primitive Church, as is seen in the New Testament, seemed to believe that David was the author of the psalter as it was known then. It is not until the second century A.D., however, that we get a clear-cut statement of Davidic authorship, in a beraitha in *Baba Bathra*.[2] At Qumrân there was no doubt whatever that David wrote Ps 151; there was little or no doubt that he was the author of the psalter as they knew it.

The second point of the LXX superscription, that the psalm is supernumerary, is lacking in Q for what would seem to be similar reasons: Ps 151 in 11QPs[a] is in no wise supernumerary. Far from being a 'rider' or something extra it is placed, with the psalm that follows it, in a climactic position to the whole scroll. The third point of the LXX superscription, that the psalm relates the Goliath episode, is the most significant of all in its absence from the Q superscription. Our psalm says nothing of that episode.

Vv. 1 and 2 of LXX correspond very closely to vv. 1 and *2a* in Q. However, it is clear already that the LXX is not a mere translation of Q. They appear already to be independent and yet closely related. While ἐν τῷ οἴκῳ might conceivably be a good translation of מבני certainly LXX v. *1c* and Q v. *1b* are so independent as to require no comment. LXX v. 2 and Q v. *2a* reconverge with only the word ἥρμοσαν lacking its counterpart in Q.

Vv. *2b* and 3 in Q, however, offer a text of which the LXX knows nothing and in which LXX and Q are totally independent. Q v. 4 reflects a theme very similar to that in LXX v. 3.

(1) Only in Ps 147 (which is lacking in 11QPs[a]) is it integral to the text of the psalm. Cf. Oesterley, *The Psalms*, i (1939), p. 19.

(2) Cf. Briggs, *The Book of Psalms* (ICC), i (1906), pp. liv–lv.

Q vv. 5*a* and 7*a* are very close to LXX v. 4, and Q vv. 5*b* and 6 relate vaguely to LXX v. 5. Finally, however, Q ends with a sentence which again has no correspondence in LXX, and, as noted above, LXX vv. 6 and 7 are lacking in QPs 151 A.

Clearly we are here dealing with a Hebrew text of Ps 151 which demands attention on its own ground. The above comparisons between the two psalms are interesting and, in some measure, revealing, but they are also manifestly limited. Not only does 11QPs 151 stand by itself, far from needing the LXX to understand it, on the contrary it comes to the aid of a correct understanding of LXX. It is quite clear that the enigmatic LXX v. 3 is wholly dependent on Q v. 4. The strange question 'Who can tell my Lord?' in the LXX means, with Q, 'Who can tell [or recount] the deeds of the Lord?' And the equally strange 'The Lord himself, he himself hears' means, with Q, that the deeds of a God who is omniscient can never be amply praised. A gross case of haplography (and misunderstanding) has taken place in the transition between Q v. 4 and LXX v. 3, i.e. between כי מי יגיד—*καὶ τίς ἀναγγελεῖ* and הוא שמע—*αὐτὸς εἰσακούει.*[1]

The first question dispensed with is whether the LXX psalm is a translation of Q. The answer is No. The next question is whether QPs 151 represents the Hebrew original ('Ur-Vorlage'?) of LXX. Is QPs 151 but a derived form of an earlier Hebrew Ps 151, or, conversely, is LXX Ps 151 a translation of an earlier or later, and hence different, Hebrew text than that we now have? Both questions are pertinent since the date of the present form of the LXX translation of the psalter is at best uncertain. While the Greek version of I Maccabees seems to quote Ps 78 (79)[2] (I Macc 7[17]), which would take us back at least to the first century B.C., we cannot be at all certain that Ps 151 was included in the Greek psalter of that time. On the contrary, though Codex Alexandrinus has, besides Ps 151, Athanasius' letter to Marcellinus which speaks freely of the psalm as Davidic, and though Codex Sinaiticus includes it as integral to the psalter, still Codex Alexandrinus carefully excludes it from belonging to the psalter proper. Furthermore, the judgement of the Laodicene canon (*βίβλος ψαλμῶν ἑκατὸν πεντήκοντα*) is sustained by the superscriptions in all the Greek manuscripts, which, though they call the psalm an *ἰδιόγραφος* of David, also call it supernumerary.[2]

Though LXX Ps 151 is by no means a translation of QPs 151, it is abundantly clear that it depends ultimately on the latter. The LXX psalter is highly compatible with MT. Where the 36 canonical psalms of 11QPs differ from MT, except in a few readings, it also differs from LXX. Q variants, in other words, for the most part stand alone. Save for a certain number of very interesting readings a general equation is possible: 11QPs^a = MT = LXX. Since there is, of course, no MT for Ps 151, one might expect that one could still retain the equation 11QPs^a = LXX for our psalm, but, as we have seen, that is far from the case.

QPs 151 includes every thought and every phrase which are in LXX Ps 151 except for LXX vv. 6 and 7, the Goliath episode. Excluding vv. 6 and 7, then, and limiting our reading of LXX Ps 151 to vv. 1–5, we make, I think, an interesting discovery: LXX Ps 151$^{1-5}$ makes little or no sense at all. V. 1 establishes that David was young and a shepherd. V. 2 says he made musical instruments, but he does nothing with them. V. 3 is so cryptic that it is very nearly meaningless. V. 4, then, is the climax but it is followed by the very anticlimactic v. 5.

If we turn to QPs 151 every objection to its counterpart in LXX listed above vanishes. The musical instruments are for rendering God glory (v. 2*b*). Nature, the mountains, and the hills

(1) The Syriac is very indefinite, 'Who will show me my Lord? He, the Lord, has become my God.' Wright, *op. cit.*, p. 264; Mingana, *Woodbrooke Studies*, i, p. 289; Spoer, *op. cit.*, p. 67; Noth, *op. cit.*, p. 8.

(2) Cf. Swete, *An Introduction to the Old Testament in Greek* (1914), pp. 252–3.

do not witness to God, but trees and animals fully appreciate David's consummate abilities (v. 3). Who of all creation, even man, however, can truly recount the deeds of the Lord? For God sees and hears everything. Moreover, he is a God who heeds (v. 4). So he sent his prophet Samuel to anoint the humble shepherd and musician (v. 5*a*). David's brothers had obvious gifts: beauty, stature, and fine hair; but, *mirabile dictu*, God chose them not (vv. 5*b* and 6)! And so the sum of it is that God took David from behind the flock and anointed him who had been רועה and מושל of sheep and goats to be נגיד and מושל of his people and the sons of his covenant (v. 7). Why? Not because David killed Goliath, that has nothing to do with it either in Q or LXX, but because David had said in his soul, 'Let me render glory unto the Lord', and with his home-made lyre he did so, still realizing that God is above all praise.

There can be no hesitancy whatever in affirming that 11QPs 151 is the original psalm. There can be no doubt, furthermore, that it is what lies behind the otherwise meaningless LXX vv. 1–5.

But where, then, did LXX vv. 6 and 7 come from? At the bottom of the column which contains QPs 151, and starting in the line following the psalm, but with almost a whole line left blank, fully indicating that Ps 151 A was finished and complete, there begins another composition. Of the latter there are only two poorly preserved lines.[(1)]

PSALM 151 B

	LXX	Q		Col. XXVIII Lines
152^{6}	ἐξῆλθον εἰς συνάντησιν τῷ ἀλλοφύλῳ	תחלת גב[ו]רה ל[דו]יד משמשחו נביא אלוהים		13
	καὶ ἐπικατηράσατό με ἐν τοῖς εἰδώλοις αὐτοῦ	אזי רׄאׄ[י]תי פלשתי	(1)	13–14
7	ἐγὼ δὲ σπασάμενος τὴν παρ' αὐτοῦ μάχαιραν	מחרף ממׄ[ערכות פלשתים]		
	ἀπεκεφάλισα αὐτόν, καὶ ἦρα ὄνειδος ἐξ υἱῶν 'Ισραήλ	...אנוכי.....את....	(2)	14

At the beginning of David's power after the prophet of God had anointed him.

1. Then I [saw] a Philistine
   uttering defiances from the r[anks of the Philistines].
2. ....I................the.......

Superscription (xxviii 13):

גב[ו]רה. The *gimel* and *bet* are without question. The left top hook of the *resh* is clear enough as well as the *he* that follows. Considering the sizes of the letters adjacent to the lacuna there is room enough, and exactly so, for the *waw* and the beginning of the *resh*. The word is further indicated by the recommendation of David given to Saul in I Sam 16^{18} ידע נגן וגבור חיל, which falls in the linking paragraph between the two stories, David's anointment and his battle with Goliath, as told in I Sam 16 and 17. David attained the strength of manhood to fight the giant because at his anointing the spirit of God had come mightily upon him, I Sam 16^{13} וימשח אתו...ותצלח רוח יהוה אל דוד. Hence the superscription to the second psalm links it as sequel to the first.

V. 1 (l. 13):

אזי. Cf. Ps 124^{3-5}.

רׄאׄ[י]תי. This reading is less secure. The תי... is without question. Preceding it are the traces of two of three letters. A search through the biblical account brings us logically to I Sam 17^{23-25}. After David had arrived in camp,

(1) Cf. 2Q22, an Apocryphon of David, found also in 4Q, and Pseudo-Philo's *Liber Antiquitatum Biblicarum*, lix (Guido Kisch ed., pp. 259–60). Note, as well, the title 'Psaume de David quand il lutta avec Goliath' (in Codex xxxv) listed in the *Catalogue de la Bibliothèque Syro-Chaldéenne du Couvent de Notre-Dame des Semences près d'Alqoš (Iraq)*, by Jacques Vosté, O.P. (1929), p. 16.

deposited his burden of provisions for his brothers, and greeted them, the giant came forth once more, and David witnessed the humiliation of all Israel. All attempts to re-establish the text on the basis of LXX vv. 6–7 fail. Furthermore, since it is clear that the latter are but an epitome of the Q psalm, there is no basis for thinking that the epitomist used the superscription or first verse of the second Q psalm in his amalgam. Rather, the second Q psalm begins at the crucial and logical point: 'Then I saw a Philistine....' The fact that אנוכי falls, isolated, in the following line supports the first-person reading. Like the psalm preceding, the psalm here is in the first person. If there were a preposition prefixed to פלשתי then many possibilities would be available, but there is none. Given the text as it stands where it is clear, ראיתי seems indicated.

V. 1 (l. 14):

מחרף. The top tracings of the letters are clear enough to entertain no doubt about the reading. If we revert again to the biblical text, a pertinent form of חרף is indicated, a verb used five times in I Sam 17 and occurring in v. 25, which is crucial for the reading ראיתי above.

ממ]ערכות פלשתים]. The first two letters are both *mem*. A search of the biblical text renders the reading almost mandatory. I Sam 17[8, 10, 23, 45]; cf. 17[26, 36]. Cf. also 1QM iii 7 *et passim*.

The reading is tenuous indeed, but there is enough to suggest that the psalm tells of the Goliath episode. If that is the case it was probably the origin of LXX vv. 6 and 7.

At some time in the history of Ps 151 an amalgamation took place between the first psalm, which dealt only with David's musicianship and anointment, and the composition which follows it. They were originally separate entities, however, and became combined at great expense to the original meaning as well as to the beauty and simplicity of at least the first of the two psalms.

Both psalms are based on I Sam 16 and 17. Only the section in Q which is totally lacking in LXX is non-biblical in tone, namely vv. 2*b*–3. The epitomist omitted them altogether whereas he has at least some salient phrase from every other verse. 11QPs 151 2*b*–3 is most revealing. The tone is quite non-biblical; the Old Testament clearly speaks of mountains and hills witnessing to God (cf. e.g. Micah 6[1]).[(1)] Trees and animals cherish David's music but they cannot themselves praise God. They can appreciate but they cannot express appreciation. A picture of mute animals and trees being charmed by music from the lyre comes to mind and with such a picture the myth of Orpheus.

The overall image of David conveyed by the psalm in Q is that of a good and pious shepherd chosen by Samuel, not for his handsomeness, but for his humility and beauty of soul. 'And [so] have I rendered glory to the Lord, thought I, within my soul.' His brothers are handsome of figure and appearance, tall, with splendid hair. David, by contrast, is a small, humble shepherd whose shepherd's music is appreciated by no one save his dumb flock and the trees among which they graze. Unattractive and a lonely figure, fully unappreciated save by nature, David none the less says in his soul that he has rendered glory to God. Such virtue of soul would have been fully appreciated in the hellenistic world. According to Josephus, God told Samuel (cf. I Sam 16[7]), 'I make not the kingdom a prize for comeliness of body, but for virtue of soul, and I seek one who in full measure is distinguished by this, one adorned with piety, justice, fortitude and obedience, qualities whereof beauty of soul consists.'[(2)]

Father J.-P. Audet has called attention to the influence of Orphism on the 'good shepherd'

(1) For recent discussions of the question of nature witnessing to or for God in the Old Testament cf. George Mendenhall, *Law and Covenant in Israel and the Ancient Near East* (1955); B. Gemser, 'The *Rîb*- or Controversy-Pattern in Hebrew Mentality', Supplements to *Vetus Testamentum*, iii (1955), pp. 120–37; H. B. Huffmon, 'The Covenant Lawsuit in the Prophets', *Journal of Biblical Literature*, lxxviii (1959), pp. 285–95. Professor van der Woude, who is at present working with Professor van der Ploeg on the Job targum from Cave 11, tells me that the Aramaic translation of Job 38[7] interprets the stars in that passage as shining instead of singing. This seems to him to indicate demythologization.

(2) The cardinal Platonic-Stoic virtues. *Antiquities*, vi. 160 (Loeb ed., pp. 246–7).

theme as it applies to Christ in early Christian literature and art.[1] Certainly David is the prototype in the New Testament of the good shepherd. That hellenistic Judaism arrogated Orpheus to monotheism for apologetic purposes is already well known in the work of the Alexandrian Jewish philosopher Aristobulus, *ca.* 150 B.C., as noted by Eusebius (*Praeparatio evangelica*, XIII. 12).[2] It is clear that Moses was viewed as a prototype of Orpheus. Eusebius (*Pr. ev.* IX. xxvii. 2 f.) tells of a Jew of the second century B.C., Artapanus, who insisted that Moses was Musaeus, the teacher of Orpheus. He also relates the vision of Moses (*Pr. ev.* IX. xxix. 5) as told by Ezekiel the Tragic Poet, wherein the Orphic god appears to Moses in a dream. For hellenized Judaism then to take the obvious next step of seeing in David, the musician, the Orphic talents and virtues is both logical and reasonable.

Among the archaeological artefacts which E. R. Goodenough uses is the painting above the niche in the central triptych area of the synagogue at Dura-Europos.[3] The painting is familiar. A sprawling vine reaches up above the Torah-ark niche area and on the left is a seated figure playing a lyre. Below the branches of the vine on the right appear to be two rampant fronting lions (there is some difference of opinion as to whether they were in a painting earlier than that of the lyre-playing figure). The identity of the musician has been disputed. Du Mesnil du Buisson and C. Hopkins have identified the figure with Orpheus while C. H. Kraeling and Rachel Wischnitzer have suggested David.[4] Goodenough has no doubt that the figure is Orpheus.[5] His only real question is what biblical or Jewish figure Orpheus represented at Dura. 'If Orpheus became for Christians a symbol of Christ taming the passions, he probably had been Moses or David, or some other Jewish figure, doing this for Jews when portrayed in a synagogue.'[6] 'He would certainly have been given some Jewish name like David.'[7] Goodenough refers also to other representations of Orpheus in Jewish art, in particular the figure with lyre surrounded by animals in the Jewish catacomb, Vigna Randanini, already identified as Orpheus by R. Eisler in 1925.[8]

Orpheus is very familiar in early Christian art. H. Leclercq, in his article 'Orphée' in *La Dictionnaire d'archéologie chrétienne et de liturgie*, includes no fewer than twelve illustrated representations of the Christianized Orpheus whose lyre charms both trees and animals.[9] If the painting of the good shepherd in the Christian chapel at Dura-Europos were better preserved we might see there also some vestiges of Orphic influence.[10] Certainly the most intriguing of all Christian representations of Orpheus is that in the Jerusalem mosaic found in 1901 and published the same year by M.-J. Lagrange.[11] Beneath the figure are a centaur and

[1] In *La Didachè*, Études bibliques (1958), pp. 417–28. I also wish to express appreciation to J.-P. Audet for his generosity in sharing with me the fruits of his work on Orphism not mentioned in his published works.

[2] Cf. M.-J. Lagrange, *Les Mystères: L'Orphisme* (1937), pp. 187–90, and *Le Judaïsme avant Jésus-Christ* (1931), pp. 494–523. Cf. also E. R. Goodenough, *By Light, Light* (1935), pp. 279–81. The following references to Eusebius may be found in the Gifford 1903 edition in vol. ii, pp. 258 ff., and vol. i, pp. 542 and 550 ff.

[3] E. R. Goodenough, *Jewish Symbols in the Greco-Roman Period*, vol. iii (1953), fig. 604, and vol. v (1956), figs. 117–19.

[4] Du Mesnil, *Les Peintures de la synagogue de Doura-Europos, 245–56 après J.-C.* (1939), p. 116. Hopkins, 'La Synagogue de Doura-Europos', in *Comptes rendus des séances de l'Académie des Inscriptions et Belles-Lettres*, Bulletin (April–June 1933), p. 246. Kraeling in *The Excavations at Dura-Europos*, Sixth Season (Yale) (1936), p. 370. R. Wischnitzer, *The Messianic Theme in the Paintings of the Dura Synagogue* (1948), p. 95.

[5] *Jewish Symbols*, vol. i (1953), p. 31.

[6] Ibid., vol. iv (1954), p. 36.

[7] Ibid., vol. v, p. 105.

[8] Ibid., vol. ii (1953), pp. 19 ff. Eisler, 'Orphisch-Dionysische Mysteriengedanken in der christlichen Antike', *Vorträge der Bibliothek Warburg*, 1922–3 (1925), pp. 4–5.

[9] Vol. xii (1935), pp. 2735–55.

[10] *The Excavations at Dura-Europos*, Fifth Season (1934), pp. 254–85. It is interesting to note that in the chapel there is also a painting of the Goliath episode at the moment when after the giant has fallen David prepares to sever his head—the very scene depicted in LXX Ps 151[7].

[11] 'Une Mosaïque byzantine à Jérusalem', *Revue biblique*, x (1901), pp. 435–44. Cf. *RB*, xi (1902), pp. 100 ff., for evidence of its being Christian. In *L'Orphisme*, p. 221, Lagrange is even more convinced than in the early reports

the god Pan obviously listening in rapt attention to the music from the lyre. Around the musician are various animals in different poses of arrested attention; a serpent and a salamander have even interrupted their fighting to listen. There are a number of trees and plants scattered among the animals and they too are listening to the divine music.[1] Of them all it may be said, as it is said of the trees and flocks in our psalm from Qumrân, that they appreciate the words and works of Orpheus, the good shepherd, whether he be David (Ezek 34[23–24]) or Christ (Luke 15[3–7] Matt 18[12–14]) or a combination of all three.

Orphic influence upon hellenistic Judaism, as well as upon early Christianity, is a matter of archaeological and literary record. Eusebius' sources, however, claimed the Orphic virtues only for Moses, and no archaeological inscriptional evidence to date has pointed unmistakably to David's share in the Orphic heritage. 11QPs 151 provides tenuous literary evidence of the Orphic image of David in the intertestamental period.

We now have the Hebrew psalms, at least all of the first and the beginning of the second, which lie behind the amalgam which is LXX Ps 151. The author was adept at writing archaizing classical Hebrew. But through that medium he reflected hellenistic ideas all the while taking his basic material directly from I Sam 16 and 17. We must manifestly acquaint ourselves with a hellenized Jew of the Palestine area. *It is highly doubtful, however, that the Qumrân community, in its fight against the hellenism of the Jerusalem priesthood, would have knowingly permitted distinctively hellenistic ideas to shape its essential theology; and no suggestion should be made on the basis of the supposed Orphic imagery in Ps 151 A that any facet of Orphism was consciously subscribed to by the writer of the poem or by his readers: discussions of live and dead symbolism are not provoked.*

The amalgamist or epitomist of the two Q psalms which were reduced to LXX Ps 151 managed to excise completely the Orphic elements as well as to destroy the beauty and integrity of the original. This was probably done in Hebrew before the translation into Greek was made, and it was done outside Qumrân. Memory of its original hellenism, however, may have served to exclude it altogether at Jamnia (*ca.* A.D. 90) from the canon of the Hagiographa.

* * *

The following inferences may be drawn. (A) We have the Hebrew lying behind LXX Ps 151[1–5]. With the psalm we have tentative literary evidence of an Orphic David from hellenized or hellenizing Judaism. (B) We have the bare beginnings of the Hebrew lying behind LXX Ps 151[6–7]. They were both probably written by the same author. (C) An amalgamist, or epitomist, combined the two, condensing them to the size of one alone, and hence sacrificed not only the artistry but also the sense of the one, and probably as well of the other. (D) LXX Ps 151 is a translation of the amalgam. (E) The superscription in LXX, like many others in the LXX psalter, is late, and, while the superscription in Syriac is very close to the superscription in Q, it is highly probable that all three superscriptions are independent of the psalm and of each other. (F) Finally, 11QPs[a] closes with psalms that deal with David's youth, his musicianship, his elevation to leadership of his people, and his manifest ability to carry out, with piety and courage, the responsibilities of that office. In the climactic placement of these psalms at

that the mosaic is Christian and that the Orphic figure is Christ as the good shepherd. The frontispiece to this latter work, which is a reproduction of the mosaic, is the clearest publication of it I have found.

(1) Goodenough, *op. cit.*, vol. v, p. 82, in speaking of the mosaic, misses the point of the trees and plants also listening; he also misses this in a number of his references. A close look at several of these clearly shows that the vegetation depicted is not merely for pastoral suggestion but is also listening, often in very graceful poses, as charmed by the music as are the animals. Cf. Kraeling, *op. cit.*, Final Report VIII, Part I (1956), p. 224.

the end of the scroll we have evidence enough, with the prose composition in the preceding column listing David's musical compositions, that at Qumrân David was considered the author of the psalter.

(SYRIAC) PSALM II

(11QPs^a 154)

Col. XVIII

(Vv. 1–3*a* and 17*b*–20 reconstructed from the Syriac)

				Syr Lines	Col. XVIII Lines
	בקהל רבים השמיעו תפארתו	בקול גדול פארו אלוהים	(1)	1–2	
	ועם אמונים ספרו גדולתו	ברוב ישרים פארו שמו	(2)	3–4	

(11QPs^a Col. XVIII)

				Syr Lines	Col. XVIII Lines
3/3	ולתמימים לפאר עליו	[חברו] לטובים נפשתכמה	(3)	5–6	1
	ואל תתעצלו להודיע עוזו	החבירו יחד להודיע ישעו	(4)	7–8	1–2
3/3/3		ותפארתו לכול פותאים			
3/2	נתנה חוכמה	כי להודיע כבוד יהוה	(5)	9	3
3/2	נודעה לאדם	ולספר רוב מעשיו	(6)	10	3–4
3/3	להשכיל לחסרי לבב גדולתו	להודיע לפותאים עוזו	(7)	11–12	4–5
2/2	הנדחים ממבואיה	הרחוקים מפתחיה	(8)	13–14	5–6
3/3	ותפארתו על כול מעשיו	כי עליון הואה אדון יעקוב	(9)	15–16	6–7
3/3	ירצה כמגיש מנחה	ואדם מפאר עליון	(10)	17–18	7–8
	כמקריב עתודים ובני בקר		(11)	19–21	8
	כמדשן מזבח ברוב עולות				9
3/3/3	כקטורת ניחוח מיד צדיקים				9–10
3/3	ומקהל חסידים זמרתה	מפתחי צדיקים נשמע קולה	(12)	22–23	10–11
3/3	ועל שתותמה בחבר יחדיו	על אוכלמה בשבע נאמרה	(13)	24–25	11–12
3/3	אמריהמה להודיע עוזו	שיחתם בתורת עליון	(14)	26–27	12
3/3	מכול זדים לדעתה	כמה רחקה מרשעים אמרה	(15)	28–29	13
3/3	על טובים תחמל	הנה עיני יהוה	(16)	30	13–14
3/3	מעת רעה יציל נפש[ם]	ועל מפאריו יגדל חסדו	(17)	31–32	14–15
		[ברכו את] יהוה	(18)	33–35	15
3/3/3	ומצי]ל [תמימים מיד רשעים]	גואל עני מיד זׄרׄ[ים			15–16
3/3	וׄשופט [עמים מישראל]	[מקים קרן מיע]קׄוׄבׄ	(19)	36–37	16
[3/3]	ויועד לנצח בירושלים]	[נוטה אהלו בציון	(20)	38–39	

1. With a loud voice glorify God;
   in the congregation of the many proclaim his majesty.
2. In the multitude of the upright glorify his name
   and with the faithful recount his greatness.

(11QPs[a])

3. [Bind] your souls with the good ones
   and with the pure ones to glorify the Most High.
4. Form an assembly to proclaim his salvation,
   and be not lax in making known his might
   and his majesty to all simple folk.

5. For to make known the glory of the Lord
   is Wisdom given,
6. And for recounting his many deeds
   she is revealed to man:
7. To make known to simple folk his might,
   and to explain to senseless folk his greatness,
8. Those far from her gates,
   those who stray from her portals.

9. For the Most High is the Lord of Jacob,
   and his majesty is over all his works.
10. And a man who glorifies the Most High
   he accepts as one who brings a meal offering,
11. as one who offers he-goats and bullocks,
   as one who fattens the altar with many burnt offerings,
   as a sweet-smelling fragrance from the hand of the righteous.

12. From the gates of the righteous is heard her voice,
   and from the assembly of the pious her song.
13. When they eat with satiety she is cited,
   and when they drink in community together,
14. Their meditation is on the Law of the Most High,
   their words on making known his might.
15. How far from the wicked is her word,
   from all haughty men to know her.

16. Behold the eyes of the Lord
   upon the good ones are compassionate,
17. And upon those who glorify him he increases his mercy;
   from an evil time will he deliver [their] soul.
18. [Bless] the Lord
   who redeems the humble from the hand of [strangers]
   [and deliv]ers [the pure from the hand of the wicked,]
19. [Who establishes a horn out of Ja]cob
   and a judge of [peoples out of Israel;]
20. [He will spread his tent in Zion
   and abide for ever in Jerusalem.]

Vv. 1–2 (Syr ll. 1–4):

These are reconstructed from the Syriac, as are portions of vv. 18–20. Noth's reconstruction is still basic for these lines, altered only where the Hebrew style of the extant 'Vorlage' indicates changes. פארו and תפארתו are used on the basis of the Syriac translator's use of the root ܫܒܚ for the Hebrew root פאר and its derivatives in vv. 3, 4, 9, 10, and 17. Only in v. 9*b* (Syr l. 16) did the translator depart from this otherwise consistent practice, where ܫܘܒܗܪܗ is used for תפארתו. Conversely, only once in vv. 3–18 does the translator use a derivative of the root to translate a Hebrew word derived from a root other than פאר; viz. in v. 7 (Syr l. 12) he translates גדולתו by ܠܬܫܒܘܚܬܗ. Hence, we may assume that גדולתו lies behind the Syr in v. 2 (Syr l. 4).

The rest of Noth's reconstruction of vv. 1–2 is here adopted intact. His choice of שמו as the word translated by ܫܘܒܚܗ is particularly perceptive. The Syr relates to Grk κλέος, which in LXX translates שֵׁם and שֵׁמַע.

If רבים is a correct reconstruction here then it would seem to be similar in sense to its frequent usage elsewhere in Qumrân literature. Contrast Ps III, v. 10 (xxiv 9).

V. 3 (Syr ll. 5–6):

Supply חֲברו with Noth from Syr ܫܘܬܦܘ. Cf. II Chron 20^{36}.

טובים (cf. v. 16) is unattested in other Qumrân literature. Cf. Ps 125^{4}, Prv 2^{20}, &c.

נפשֹׁתְכמה, defective plural (cf. Jer 44^{7}). Syr sing., emended to pl. by Noth *et al.* Read נפשָׁתכמה?

תמימים, cf. Ps 37^{18}, Prv 2^{21}, &c. A designation of the members of the Qumrân sect in 1QS iii 3, *et passim*; 1QM xiv 7; 1QH i 36, &c.

לפאר, cf. vv. 10 and 17. Those who join or form the assembly are those who glorify the Most High. As important as it is in this psalm the expression is unattested elsewhere in published Qumrân literature.

V. 4 (Syr ll. 7–8):

החבירו יחד (cf. Job 16^{4}), 'Form an assembly (community)'. Syr has ܐܟܚܕܐ, with Noth, יחדיו. If יחד is an appellative noun its significance escaped the Syr translator.

להודיע here and in vv. 5, 7, and 14, along with לספר in v. 6 and להשכיל in v. 7, expresses the task, purpose, or *raison d'être* of the assembly. Cf. 1QH vi 10–13 xi 9–12 xiii 12–15 xv 19–21; 1QHf **15** 4; CD xiii 7–8; and *DJD I*, 34*bis*, 3 ii 7 (p. 154). Cf. passive construction in Syr.

Syr interchanges ישעו and עוזו, and adds in Syr l. 8 a second עוזו (ܒܥܘܫܢܗ). The Syr line is hence metrically overloaded, whereas Q has a perfect 3/3/3.

פותאים. For spelling cf. 1QHf **15** 4 and 11QPs^{a} xii 3 (Ps 119^{130}). Philonenko goes far astray in taking this to mean the pious and humble of Qumrân. Whereas it does mean that in 1QpHab xii 4 and perhaps in 1QpMicah (*DJD I*, p. 78), it unmistakably means 'senseless ones' or 'fools' in 1QH ii 9, 1QSa i 19, CD xiii 6, and 1QHf **15** 4, as well as here. In v. 7 it is parallel to חסרי לבב (cf. Prv 7^{7}). A similar parallel phrase is in 1QH ii 9, where the parallel פושעים determines the sense beyond all doubt.

V. 5 (Syr l. 9):

Although Qumrân literature contains Wisdom vocabulary, the personification of Wisdom is unattested heretofore in published Qumrân literature. Cf. also xxi 11 ff. and xxvi 9 ff.

V. 7 (Syr l. 12):

חסרי לבב, cf. *supra* the note to v. 4, and the similar נמהרי לב in 1 QH ii 9.

V. 8 (Syr ll. 13–14):

מפתחיה, ממבואיה. The Syr translator rightly took these as the doors of Wisdom (cf. Prv 8^{34} $9^{1\,\text{ff.}}$ 14^{1}, Sirach 1^{15} 14^{23} $24^{8\,\text{ff.}}$).

נדחים, 'those who stray' (cf. Deut 4^{19} 22^{1} 30^{17}), parallel to הרחוקים.

N.B. The writing surface of the skin is rough and poorly prepared (scar tissue?) so that the scribe was forced to make an erasure in line 6 of Col. xviii and to leave the following two ruled lines blank (cf. Pl. XII).

V. 10 (Syr l. 17):

ירצה, cf. II Sam 24^{23}, Hos 8^{13}, Jer $14^{10,\,12}$, Ezek 20^{40-41} 43^{27}. The Almighty accepts him who glorifies God as favourably as him who offers many sacrifices (vv. 10–11). Cf. 1QS v 1 ff. ix 4 ff. and Syr. But read יֵרָצֶה?

V. 11 (Syr ll. 19–21):

N.B.: Erasure of ריח (?) in l. 9. Cf. Syr.

Note the phraseology in 1QS ix 4–5 with respect to him whose lips serve justice; he is like a pleasing (scent) of righteousness, a pure way, a vow of acceptable offering. Cf. Delcor, pp. 94–95; but see also F. M. Cross, Jr., *The Ancient Library of Qumrân* (1961), pp. 100–3.

V. 12 (Syr ll. 22–23):

מפתחי צדיקים, unattested elsewhere in Qumrân literature. Contrast the Syr in the various manuscripts (note, however, that Mosul 1113 omits the second-person pronoun suffix of the other Syr texts, more nearly approximating the Hebrew).

קולה (contrast Syr ܡܠܬܗ): the voice of Wisdom. Wisdom is with the צדיקים and חסידים for the purpose, v. 14 (cf. *supra* v. 4), of proclaiming God's might, &c. On מקהל cf. Syr.

זמרתה, 'her song', cf. Gen 43[11] (MT and LXX). Syr ll. 22–23 are the most uncertain of the whole psalm, as a comparative study of the various Syr manuscripts reveals. The synonymous parallelism as well as the perfect echoing rhythm and metre of Q v. 12 leave no doubt about its primacy. The Syr 'pointer' was not aware that the psalmist had returned to the Wisdom theme, as he shows also in Syr l. 28 (cf. *infra* v. 15). Noth *et al.*, of course, followed the translator in his error; it is but that much more amazing that Noth saw the possibility of a return to the Wisdom theme (pp. 18–19). Cf. Prv 8[1 ff.], &c. (Note that Mosul 1113 reads ܡܙܡܘܪܬܗ, 'her song'.)

V. 13 (Syr ll. 24–25):

נאמרה, cf. rabbinic כנאמר. Perhaps a reference to Wisdom's voice and song (v. 12) and/or the study and conviviality while dining (v. 14). One should not emend on the basis of Syr ܒܡܐܪܐ to נאמנה.

בחבר יחדיו (so Syr), unattested elsewhere in Qumrân literature. Cf. 1QSa ii 11–22 and 1QS vi 4 ff.

V. 14 (Syr ll. 26–27):

שיחתם (so Mosul ܡܦܚܡܬܗܘܢ), 'their meditation'. Cf. 1QS x 16, 1QH vi 11 ix 7 xi 5. See especially 1QS vi 6–7 and Isaiah Sonne's excellent comments thereon in *Vetus Testamentum*, vii (1957), pp. 405–8.

אמריהמה. At table, while eating with satiety and drinking in community, meditation is on Torah and discussions are of the task of the assembly, להודיע עוזו. Cf. *supra* v. 4, and 1QS vi 6 ff.

V. 15 (Syr ll. 28–29):

אמרה, Wisdom's word or speech. Contrast Syr pointing (l. 28).

לדעתה, to know Wisdom. Contrast Syr (l. 29) ܠܡܝܕܥܗ = לדעתו. The Syr 'pointer', unaware that the psalmist had reverted to the Wisdom theme, took these to mean the word and knowledge of God directly.

זדים, cf. 1QH vi 35.

V. 16 (Syr l. 30):

עיני . . . תחמל. Perhaps emend with Syr (ܒܥܝܢܗ) to עין; or assume the *yod* to indicate *ḥireq compaginis*.

V. 17 (Syr l. 32):

מעת רעה (Amos 5[13], Micah 2[3]). Noth, not having the Qumrân literature to guide (or misguide) him, used the biblical phrase which indeed was correct. The high eschatology of the later stages of Qumrân theology is lacking in this psalm (contrast Philonenko).

V. 18 (Syr l. 34):

ברכו את, with Noth; on the basis of Syr J. Strugnell reads ך̊[ברו].

עני, 'the humble'. Cf. 1QH ii 34 v 13–14, CD vi 16–21 xiv 14.

זרים, with Noth on the basis of Syr ܢܘܟܪܝܐ (= נכרים). Read perhaps זר or זד?

Vv. 18–20 (Syr ll. 33–39):

Again Noth's reconstruction remains basic. However, the 'Vorlage' clearly shows that participial *nomina agentis* were used in vv. 18*b*–19*a* and not finite verbs (i.e. גואל lies behind Syr ܦܪܘܩ—hence מציל and מקים may be assumed). On the basis of the general lack of the definite article in the extant text it is omitted in the reconstructions (vv. 1–2, 18–20).

11QPs[a] contains only vv. 3–17 and portions of vv. 18–19 of Ps II, which, judging from the Syriac translation, originally had twenty verses. It is essentially a poem of bicolons in 3/3 metre. Vv. 4, 11, and 18 are tricolons in 3/3/3; vv. 5 and 6 are in 3/2; v. 8 is in 2/2; and v. 12 is in 4/3. There are four bicolons of synonymous or complete parallelism (vv. 4*a*–*b*, 7, 8, and 13) and others which are very nearly so (vv. 12, 14, and 15). V. 11, the metre of which Noth failed to perceive (Syr ll. 19–21), is a tricolon continuation of v. 10, an interruption of the sense-flow of the psalm for dramatic emphasis: the man who glorifies the Most High is as favourably accepted as one who at the holy altar offers the prescribed sacrifices, and as though he himself were a sweet-smelling savour offered by the hand of the righteous.

If we count the verses reconstructed from the Syriac there are five strophes in the full psalm. The first, second, and fourth strophes have four verses each, the third three, and the fifth five. The tricolon v. 11 fills out the third strophe, however; and the final prayer in vv. 18–20 appears to be the goal of the whole psalm, the eschatological hope of a theophany on Zion.

Form-critically one thinks of a *berakhah* or a 'Call to Worship'. The first strophe contains seven imperatives, all of which are exhortations to glorify God and to proclaim his might and majesty in an assembly of the 'good' and 'pure'. It is a *Venite* (Ps 95; cf. Pss 96, 98, 100) or a *Benedicite*. It is, more generally speaking, a sapiential hymn. The second and fourth strophes proclaim the purpose of the gift of Wisdom—that the good and pure (v. 3) and the righteous and saintly (v. 12) may indeed proclaim God's deeds and greatness (vv. 6–7, 14). Neither the senseless nor the foolish have Wisdom (vv. 7–8); and the wicked and insolent certainly do not know her (v. 15). The third strophe proclaims that glorifying God and having Wisdom are as acceptable as offering many sacrifices. And the last strophe proclaims the assurance that the good, the pure, the glorifiers, and the poor, though experiencing an evil time, will surely know God's compassion, loving faithfulness, and deliverance from the hands of strangers and wicked men (vv. 16–18). The last strophe has the traits of a congregational or collective *Klagelied*. V. 18, however, reverts to the theme of the first strophe with the liturgical formula of a call to bless the Lord who is redeemer, deliverer, and sustainer.

More telling perhaps than either a poetic or a form-critical analysis of the psalm is an analysis of its contents. The first two strophes, through v. 8, are made up of a series of imperatives, complementary infinitives, direct objects of the infinitives, and indirect objects. Drawn together into their respective categories they present an impressive statement of the purpose of the calling of the assembly: '. . . Praise . . . proclaim . . . sing . . . tell . . . join . . . form an assembly; . . . to make known . . . to make known . . . to make known . . . to tell . . . to make known . . . to enlighten; . . . his salvation . . . his might . . . his majesty . . . the glory of the Lord . . . his many works . . . his might . . . his greatness; . . . to all fools . . . to fools . . . to the senseless . . . those far from her gates . . . those who stray from her doors.'

The senseless and foolish, those far from Wisdom's gates (vv. 4, 7, 8), seem to be one out of three distinct groups mentioned in the psalm. The senseless and foolish are the group at whom the proclamation of the assembly is directed. They are the ones who should get the message, hear the praise of God, and learn of his glory, greatness, and mighty deeds.

Another group is designated as the רבים . . . ישרים . . . אמונים . . . טובים . . . תמימים . . . צדיקים . . . חסידים . . . טובים . . . מפאריו . . . עני . . . תמימים (many, righteous, faithful, good, pure, righteous, saintly, good, glorifiers, poor, pure—vv. 1, 2, 3, 12, 16–18). Clearly (vv. 1–3) this is the group called to perform the service and duties listed above in the complementary infinitives. This is the group which is addressed by the 'Call to Worship', the imperatives of the first strophe. It has a task to perform, that of telling of God's deeds and greatness to the foolish and senseless. The good ones have Wisdom given them in their task of proclaiming God's might, and even reflect Wisdom's voice and song in their gates when they eat and drink in meditation on the Law and on proclaiming his might (vv. 5–7, 12–14).

But there is a third group as well, the רשעים and זדים of v. 15, and the ז̊ר̊[ים] and [רשעים] of v. 18. These, by contrast, do not have Wisdom; her word is far from them; knowledge of her is not theirs (v. 15). On the contrary, they appear to be the enemies of the good ones, doing them harm, bringing on them an evil time (vv. 17–18). It is possible, of course, because of the similarities between vv. 8 and 15 to confuse the senseless ones with the wicked ones. But actually all they have in common is their lack of Wisdom. Otherwise they are distinct groups; whereas the senseless ones are the object of the programme of proclamation by the pure and good, the wicked and insolent are not mentioned at all in that connexion, but, on the contrary, must be dealt with by God himself in the anticipated theophany (v. 18).

Of the three groups only the 'in-group' has Wisdom even though it was originally given of God to all mankind (v. 6). The language of vv. 8 and 12 reflects passages in sapiential literature wherein Wisdom is personified (Prv $8^{1\,ff.}$ 8^{34} $9^{1\,ff.}$ 14^{1}, Sirach 1^{15} 14^{23} $24^{8\,ff.}$). Wisdom's gates, her voice, and her song (vv. 8, 12) strongly suggest a doctrine of Wisdom heretofore lacking in the literature from Qumrân except for manuscripts of the sapiential literature already well known before the discoveries at Qumrân.[(1)] Although our psalm does not go beyond a poetic personification of Wisdom it exceeds in that direction not only the Qumrân literature published to date but also the canonical psalter.[(2)] In fact, the biblical psalter specifically and the Qumrân literature generally seem on about the same plane of interest in Wisdom thinking. Save for material in 11QPs[a], there is no personification, and certainly no hypostatization, of Wisdom in Qumrân literature, even though there is ample enough Wisdom vocabulary (e.g. חכם, בין, שכל, and their derivatives), especially in 1QS and 1QH.[(3)] Exactly the same is true of the canonical psalter.[(4)]

The content of the psalm, therefore, reveals three distinct groups, one of which is called, in assemblage or community, to a programme of proclamation directed toward another of the groups. The third group, the wicked, stands over against the other two as perpetrators of an evil time and as enemies of the 'in-group', those called into assembly.

A literary analysis of the vocabulary and idioms of the psalm yields no results whatever that would be helpful in suggesting a *Sitz im Leben*, provenance, or date for the psalm. The vocabulary of the psalm is biblical. While certain phrases do not occur as such in the Bible, all the words and ideas are potentially biblical (cf. the notes above to vv. 3 ff.).

In other words, there is nothing of necessity Qumrânian in the psalm.[(5)] And yet it is

(1) Cf. 'Le Travail d'édition des fragments manuscrits de Qumrân', *Revue biblique*, lxiii (1956), and especially p. 54 (communication de M. Baillet), the fragments of Sirach (6^{20-31}) in Hebrew. This notice gave rise to a number of articles on the relation of Sirach to the Qumrân literature, especially those of M. R. Lehmann and J. Carmignac in *Revue de Qumrân*, Nos. 9 and 10, February (pp. 103–16) and May (pp. 209–18) 1961. A series of articles had appeared earlier on the relation of Wisdom of Solomon to the Qumrân literature: A.-M. Dubarle, 'Une Source du livre de la Sagesse?', *Revue des sciences philosophiques et théologiques*, xxxvii (1953), pp. 431 ff.; M. Delcor, 'L'Immortalité de l'âme dans la Sagesse et à Qumrân', *Nouvelle Revue théologique*, lxxvii (1955), pp. 614 ff.; and M. Philonenko, 'Le Maître de justice et la Sagesse de Salomon', *Theologische Zeitschrift*, xiv (1958), pp. 81 ff. But no work has been done, to my knowledge, on Wisdom thinking generally in Qumrân literature. Note also the sapiential flavour in 1Q26 (*Discoveries in the Judaean Desert*, i, p. 102), other copies of which have come from Cave 4 and are in the hands of Professor John Strugnell; cf. *Revue biblique*, lxiii (1956), p. 64. For Sirach $51^{13\,ff.}$ and another sapiential poem cf. Cols. xxi and xxvi, *infra* pp. 79 ff. and 89 f.

(2) For working definitions of personification and hypostatization cf. Helmer Ringgren, *Word and Wisdom* (1947), p. 8, and the correctives offered by Ralph Marcus, 'On Biblical Hypostases of Wisdom', *Hebrew Union College Annual*, xxiii (1950–1), Part I, pp. 157 ff. Marcus was right to point out that Wisdom in late biblical literature is essentially and uniformly a poetic personification, not an hypostasis leading to the creation of an independent deity (pp. 166–7).

(3) Carmignac, *Revue de Qumrân*, No. 10, p. 217, n. 6, rightly notes that whereas חכם is used in Sirach, שכל is preferred at Qumrân.

(4) Of all the psalter, Ringgren (*op. cit.*, p. 132) cites only Ps 104^{24} as comparable to such passages as Prv 3^{19} and Jer 10^{12}, God's creating the world by Wisdom (cf. xxvi 13 ff.).

(5) טובים is unattested elsewhere in known Qumrân literature as an adjective referring to pious men. The root פאר, so dominant in this psalm, occurs only in 1QH xiii 17 (cf. notes above to v. 3). Such a phrase as פתחי צדיקים is unattested elsewhere in Qumrân literature (cf. note to v. 12). And as already stressed, 11QPs[a] is so far unique at Qumrân in its language of the personification of Wisdom (cf. notes to v. 5).

inevitable that one should think of Qumrân in dealing with the psalm. Vv. 13 and 14 reflect many passages in 1QS, the common meals of the settlement, the life of sacramental eating and drinking accompanied by meditation and discussion of the Law, and the task of the covenanted people (cf. 1QS vi 4 ff., and notes above). תמימים is attested many times as designating the members of the sect.(1)

The most arresting phrase in the psalm is החבירו יחד. If the hif'il is read for the verb and יחד is read as a noun then the translation could range from 'Form an assembly' to 'Form a *yaḥad*'. If the latter translation could be established then we would be faced with the difficulty of having in this psalm the first such phrase at Qumrân. In this case the psalm might be more than a 'Call to Worship'; it might then be considered a poetic reflection on the founding of a particular group having the particular purpose of proclaiming God's might, &c. (first strophe) to those who lack Wisdom.

The language of the psalm, as already noted, is not yet the language definitely peculiar to Qumrân. The eschatology of the psalm is not yet the fully developed eschatology familiar in the *pesharim*, 1 and 4QM, 1QH, 1QS, 1QSa, CD, and other Qumrân literature. The eating and drinking of v. 13 may reflect a sacral, eschatological meal, and the hope expressed in the fifth strophe seems eschatological, but the vocabulary of high eschatology is lacking.(2) There is no great leader here. One receives the impression of a group which is still seeking its identity and is still concerned with its *regroupement* and its *raison d'être*. And if we may revert to a facet of the first observation, the language is archaic, or archaizing. For it to have been accepted in the Qumrân psalter, it was probably considered ancient enough to merit a place alongside the thirty-six psalms in the scroll which later at Jamnia were deemed canonical. If its actual date were known, or if its author were remembered, it probably would not have been included in 11QPs^{a}, which at Qumrân was clearly considered a portion of the Davidic psalter.

The psalm may perhaps be proto-Essenian, or Ḥasidic, from the period of the 'separation' of the dissident group, an early poetic expression of the 'calling out' of the sect and of its *raison d'être* as it was then understood.

(SYRIAC) PSALM III

(11QPs^{a} 155)

Col. XXIV, ll. 3–17

					Syr Lines	Col. XXIV Lines
2/2	הקשיבה אלי		יהוה קראתי אליכה	(1)	1	3
2/2	למעון קודשכה		פרשתי כפי	(2)	2	3–4
2/2	ותן לי את שאלתי		הט אוזנכה	(3)	3–4	4
2/2	אל תמנע ממני		ובקשתי	(4)	5	4–5
2/2	ואל תמגרה		בנה נפשי	(5)	6	5
2/2	לפני רשעים		ואל תפרע	(6)	7	5–6
2/2/2	דין האמת	ישיב ממני	גמולי הרע	(7)	8	6

(1) Cf. 1QS iv 22, 1QM xiv 7, 1QH i 36, &c., and Paul Kahle, *The Cairo Geniza* (1959), p. 98.

(2) The expressions בקץ הרשעה (1QpHab v 7), קץ אחרון (1QpHab vii 7, 12, 1 QS iv 16), and עת צרה (as it is used in 1QM i 11 and xv 1) have distinctly heavy eschatological meanings. עת רעה in our v. 17, however, may mean no more than it means in Amos 5^{13} and Micah 2^{3}. Contrast Delcor (p. 92) and Philonenko (p. 41).

				Syr Lines	Col. XXIV Lines
3/3	כי לוא יצדק לפניכה כול חי	יהוה אל תשפטני כחטאתי	(8)	9–10	6–7
3/3	ואת משפטיכה למדני	הבינני יהוה בתורתכה	(9)	11–12	8
3/3	ועמים יהדרו את כבודכה	וישמעו רבים מעשיכה	(10)	13–14	9
3/3	ואל תביאני בקשות ממני	זכורני ואל תשכחני	(11)	15–16	10
3/3	ופשעי אל יזכרו לי	חטאת נעורי הרחק ממני	(12)	17–18	11
3/3	ואל יוסף לשוב אלי	טהרני יהוה מנגע רע	(13)	19–20	12
3/3	ואל ינצו ע[ל]יו בי	יבש שורשיו ממני	(14)	21–22	12–13
3/3	על כן שאלתי מלפניכה שלמה	כבוד אתה יהוה	(15)	23–24	13–14
3/3	ובני אדם מה יוסיף אומ[צם]	למי אזעקה ויתן לי	(16)	25–26	14–15
	קראתי יהוה ויענני	מׄלפׄ[נ]יכה יהוה מבטחי	(17)	27–28	15–16
3/3/3		[וירפא את] שבר לבי		29	16
	חלמתי גם [הקיצותי]	נמתי [ואי]שנה	(18)	30	16–17
	ואקרא] יהוה [מפלטי]	[סמכתני יהוה הוכה לבי	(19)	31–33	17
	חסיתי בכה ולוא אבוש]	[עתה אראה בושתם	(20)	34–35	
	ובית יעקוב בחיריכה]	[פדה את ישראל חסידיכה יהוה	(21)	37–38	

1. O Lord, I called unto thee, give heed to me.
2. I spread forth my palms toward thy holy dwelling.
3. Incline thine ear and grant me my plea,
4. And my request withhold not from me.
5. Edify my soul and do not cast it down
6. And abandon (it) not in the presence of the wicked.
7. May the Judge of Truth remove from me the rewards of evil.
8. O Lord, judge me not according to my sins;
   for no man living is righteous before thee.
9. Grant me understanding, O Lord, in thy Law,
   and teach me thine ordinances,
10. That many may hear of thy deeds
    and peoples may honour thy glory.
11. Remember me and forget me not,
    and lead me not into situations too hard for me.
12. The sins of my youth cast far from me,
    and may my transgressions be not remembered against me.
13. Purify me, O Lord, from (the) evil scourge
    and let it not turn again upon me.
14. Dry up its roots from me
    and let its leaves not flourish within me.
15. Thou art (my) glory, O Lord.
    Therefore is my request fulfilled before thee.

16. To whom may I cry and he would grant (it) me?
    And the sons of man—what more can [their] pow[er] do?—
17. My trust, O Lord, is befo[r]e thee.
    I cried, 'O Lord', and he answered me,
    [and he healed] my broken heart.
18. I slumbered [and sl]ept,
    I dreamt; indeed [I awoke.]
19. [Thou didst support me, O Lord, when my heart was smitten]
    [and I invoked] the Lord, [my deliverer.]

(From the Syriac)

Syr
Lines

[20.] 34. Now shall I behold their shame;
35. I have trusted in thee and shall not be abashed.
36. (Render glory for ever and ever.)
[21.] 37. Deliver Israel, O Lord, thy faithful ones,
38. and the house of Jacob, thy chosen ones.

V. 1 (Syr l. 1):
ܡܪܝܐ is lacking in Wright's Cambridge MS. In Q יהוה is an anacrusis, falling outside the metre, a vocative cry serving the whole first strophe.

V. 2 (Syr l. 2):
פרשתי, with Mosul.
למעון קודשכה, cf. 1QS viii 8, 1QM xii 2, 1QSb iv 25 (*DJD I*, p. 126). Syr מעוני.

V. 3 (Syr l. 4):
שאֶלתי, Ming 51, Cambridge and Berlin MSS. read sing. with Q. לי > Mosul.

V. 4 (Syr l. 5):
ובַקָּשָׁתִי receives two stresses in the metre. *Waw* > Syr.

V. 6 (Syr l. 7):
J. Strugnell reads תִּפָּרַע, 'let it not be denuded'.

V. 7 (Syr l. 8):
The Syr is very nearly verbatim Q, also 2/2/2. The whole first strophe of Syr is metrically the same as Q, especially if יהוה in l. 1 is viewed as a vocative anacrusis. The metre serves the purpose of the staccato cries of the falsely accused. Syr השיב.
דַּיַּן האמת, following Syr.

V. 8 (Syr l. 9):
כחטאתַי, read (defective) pl. with Syr. Cf. v. 12.

V. 8 (Syr l. 10):
Mosul 1113 has ܕܚܝ (חי) rather than the ܟܠ of the other Syr texts. (Cf. 1QS iv 26 *et passim*, 1QH ix 14 ff. xv 22, CD xii 21.) Delcor was right in referring to Ps 143[2].

V. 9 (Syr ll. 11–12):
An alphabetic acrostic seems to begin, with ה, at this point. See discussion below.

V. 10 (Syr l. 13):
רבים is here parallel to עמים and does not have the significance it has in 1QS vi, &c. Cf. Isa 52[14].

V. 11 (Syr l. 16):
בקשות ממני, cf., with Philonenko, Matt 6[13].
Noth failed to translate Syr ܡܢܝ (Q ממני) in his Hebrew reconstruction, but has it in the German.

V. 12 (Syr ll. 17–18):

חטאת, read (defective) pl. with Syr and in parallelism to פשעי in v. 12*b*; cf. *supra* v. 8.

פשעי, Syr ܣܘܪ̈ܚܢܘܗܝ. Cf. Mosul. Noth was certainly not far wrong in choosing עונותי on the basis of the Syr readings of Ps 18[36]. Philonenko went far afield in seeing in the Syr a reference to the suffering of the Teacher of Righteousness.

V. 13 (Syr l. 20):

לשוב, with Mosul.

The *yod* of אלי is superscribed and half obliterated by a worm hole.

V. 14 (Syr ll. 21–22):

יֵבֵשׁ, with Syr, and parallel to v. 13.

ינצו, from נצץ, 'to blossom'; cf. Mosul ܢܦܪܚܘܢ.

עליו, 'its leaves' as in Ezek 17[7], from Syr ܛܪ̈ܦܘܗܝ (cf. Ezek 17[9]). Certainly some image such as that of the eagle and the branches of Ezek 17 lies behind this verse. But here the image is internalized and the roots and leaves, while remaining metaphors, refer to what sin does inside a man. J. Strugnell reads עחיו and P. Skehan ענפיו; but cf. Ps 32[5].

V. 15 (Syr l. 23):

כבוד, Syr ܟܒܝܪܐ read כביר (cf. Job 36[5]). Cf. Ps 3[4]. The *Danklied*, suggested in vv. 1–2, is here resumed.

V. 16 (Syr l. 26):

אומ[צם], cf. Job 17[9]. V. 16*b* is an anacoluthon. So J. Strugnell.

V. 17 (Syr l. 27):

מלפ[נ]יכה, see Syr ܡܢ ܩܕܡܝܟ.

Vv. 15–17 (Syr ll. 23–29):

The psalmist's request and trust are both מלפניכה in vv. 15 and 17, reflecting the *Danklied* framework of the whole psalm. V. 16 recapitulates the thrust of the *Klagelied* (vv. 3–14) which is embedded in the *Danklied* (vv. 1–2, 15 ff.; cf. Noth, pp. 15–16).

Vv. 17–18 (Syr ll. 27–31):

These verses are easily reconstructed on the basis of the Syr translation and Ps 3[4–6].

יהוה is a quotation (I called, 'O Lord') referring back to the *Klagelied* (cf. יהוה in vv. 1, 8, 9, 13). V. 17*b* begins an address to the 'congregation' similar to that in Ps 22[24 ff.], and follows the account of God's answer to the request of the falsely accused (cf. v. 15*b* and Ps 22[22b]; cf. Sanders, *Suffering as Divine Discipline* (1955), pp. 92 and 104).

V. 19 (Syr ll. 31–33):

The psalmist reverts to the prayer form of the *Danklied* (cf. Ps 22[26]).

Vv. 20–21 (Syr ll. 34–38):

I am indebted to P. W. Skehan for much of the reconstruction of these verses, which is based on the available Syr readings and the necessary alphabetic sequence. Syr l. 36 is a late doxology?

Noth (p. 15) is right in seeing in this psalm an overall *individuelles Danklied* with a *Klagelied*, a prayer of the falsely accused, embedded in it (vv. 3–14, Syr ll. 3–27). הקשיבה אלי in v. 1 and יהוה in v. 17*b* are quotations of what the psalmist had cried out in his time of trouble. Vv. 1 and 2, and 15 ff., clearly indicate that the psalm was written after divine help and healing had been effected. There is no superscription in either Syr or Q.

The first strophe of seven verses is predominantly in 2/2 metre, with the seventh verse a 2/2/2. The vocative יהוה in v. 1 is an anacrusis. The Syriac translation retains these 2/2 metres except in ll. 3 and 4 (see notes above). Noth is led astray in his Hebrew translation into seeking a 4/4 or 3/3 metre, hence his difficulty in v. 4 (Syr l. 5) and his various efforts to gain beats by using separable prefixes and suffixes.

The second strophe of seven verses (Syr ll. 9–22) is in 3/3. The first strophe is composed of staccato pleas uttered manifestly in desperation and despair. They are the cries of a man in dire straits, uttered in clipped and pitiful tones. The second strophe is of a quite different movement. The wronged man stands before God asking that justice be mitigated and that his suffering be turned to an experience of learning God's Law (vv. 9–10). If he be spared the psalmist will proclaim God's ways and deeds to many (cf. Ps $22^{23\text{ ff.}}$). He begs to be cleansed of his scourge and not to be led into temptation (v. 11*b*). The staccato cries for God's attention of the first strophe are here transformed into pleas for forgiveness, mercy, and purity.

The third strophe resumes the *Danklied*, which had only been suggested in v. 2, telling of God's fulfilment of the psalmist's request: he called and God answered and healed. Judging from the Syriac translation, the third strophe, like the first two, would also have had seven verses.

The psalm appears to be a broken or imperfect alphabetic acrostic. Starting at v. 9, the verses begin with sequential letters of the Hebrew alphabet commencing with ה. Whether or not the last verses, represented in Syr ll. 32–38, continued the alphabetic sequence is difficult to determine; the corresponding Syriac lines do not afford enough text to work on. If the metre of the third strophe was maintained to the end of the psalm, there would have been eight more two-colon verses (ט–ת), and the Syriac would have to be considered deficient. Col. xxiv has seventeen lines of text and could originally have run for eight or nine more lines: barely, though possibly, enough to contain eight more verses of Ps III and the first four lines of Ps 142, which continues at v. 5 on Col. xxv l. 1. The greatest difficulty in assuming such to be the case is that the Hebrew and Syriac present almost rigidly parallel texts as far as the Hebrew is preserved in 11QPs^a.

Another difficulty in assuming that the Hebrew text maintained the alphabetic arrangement through ת is in the observation that the first strophe of 11QPs No. III is not so constructed. While the initial ב of v. 5 might conceivably represent an alphabetization of the text, the ג of גמולי and the ד of דין, both in v. 7, do not introduce sequential verses. For them to do so, there would have to be four colons in the ב verse (2/2/2/2), two in the ג verse (2/2), and three in the ד verse (3/2/4?). Furthermore, דין is clearly a noun (cf. Syr l. 8) and not a verb, as one would construe it otherwise. Where the alphabetic arrangement is clear, in vv. 9 ff., the metric structure is quite regular and certainly not as 'interesting' as such a structure would be in the first eight verses. On the contrary the Syriac translation fully indicates the metric and strophic arrangement here offered (but see P. Skehan in *The Catholic Biblical Quarterly*, xxvii [1965], pp. 1 ff.).

What there is of the alphabetic versification commences at ה, in v. 9, and continues, at least, through ל in v. 16. And the alphabetic arrangement of vv. 17–19 is inescapable; despite the resultant interruption of the sense-flow at v. 17*b*, v. 19*a* resumes the direct address to God of v. 17*a*, which then continues to the end of the psalm in the Syriac version. Reversification of the constituent colons of the extant third strophe along lines other than that of the indicated alphabetic arrangement would be but arbitrary.

The above observations, however, do not resolve the problem, already noted, of how far the alphabetic versification was followed in the remaining portion of the psalm lacking in the scroll. The psalm does not commence alphabetically; on the basis of the Syriac it seems to have terminated short of ת. It is at best an imperfect alphabetic acrostic.

Ps No. III, in contrast to No. II, gives rise to no hypothesis of proto-Essenian provenance.

A. At every point where Delcor and Philonenko saw Essenian elements in the Syriac translation of No. III the Hebrew original fails to support their contentions, at least not to the exclusion of other possible explanations. At Syr l. 10 (Q v. 8), where Philonenko saw the reference to the Qumrân doctrine of sinful flesh, supposing an original Hebrew כול בשר, Q has כול חי, verbatim Ps 143[2b] (MT and 11QPs[a] Col. xxv). At Syr l. 18 (Q v. 12), where Philonenko saw a reference to the righteous suffering of the Teacher of Righteousness, supposing an original Hebrew מוסר, Q has פשעי!

B. While a number of words and phrases, and even ideas in the psalms, are also met with in other Qumrân literature (cf. notes to vv. 2, 8, 15, 16) these same expressions are also typically biblical. Where, e.g., Philonenko sees in Syr ll. 11–14 (Q vv. 9–10) a parallel to 1QH vi 10–13, an image of the Teacher of Righteousness praying for instruction from God that he might in turn instruct others, we must surely admit that many psalmists and men of faith from biblical times on have uttered the same prayer. Furthermore, 11QPs[a] in its entirety is attributed to David. A psalm known to have been written by the Teacher of Righteousness would not at Qumrân have been attributed to David!

Ps No. II, in contrast to No. III, could be proto-Essenian. Many cross-references can and should be made on the basis of No. II to other Qumrân literature (cf. *supra* the notes to No. II). Of the three Syriac non-canonical psalms for which in 11QPs[a] we now have the Hebrew originals or 'Vorlagen', only No. II is possibly Qumrânian in theology or phraseology. No. I, or Ps 151, is surely non-Qumrânian in origin.[(1)] And No. III, it now appears, is as 'biblical' as Ps 22 itself, being a combination of two biblical *Gattungen*, the *Danklied* and the *Klagelied*.

The fact that the three psalms appear in 11QPs[a] says nothing about their ultimate origin. Certainly no one will suggest that the thirty-six canonical psalms were penned at Qumrân! Furthermore, the three are interspersed among the thirty-six canonicals (in Cols. xviii, xxiv, and xxviii) in such a way as to cast no doubt on their 'canonicity' at Qumrân, or to suggest any relationship among them. They have no more special relationship of origin one to another than do Pss 141, 133, and 144, which in 11QPs[a] appear (in that order) on the same column.

Clearly the answer as to why the psalms appear together in the various Syriac manuscripts must be sought elsewhere than at Qumrân. It was clear before the recovery of 11QPs[a] that the superscriptions in Syriac were late as well as forced. They bear little or no relation to the psalms themselves. They are totally without value in any discussion of the provenance or date of the individual psalms. They offer little enough explanation as to why they were grouped together by Syrian Christians, except that Nos. I, IV, and V seem to deal with David's various altercations as a shepherd lad. If Nos. IV and V also emerge from the Qumrân caves in another scroll or group of fragments then there will be reason enough to discuss a possible discovery of the cave materials in the ninth or tenth centuries by Syrian Christians or some other group, such as the Karaites, from whom they may have learned of these psalms.[(2)] The greatest obstacle to such a theory is that Syr Ps No. I is clearly a translation of LXX Ps 151 and not of 11QPs 151.

11QPs No. III is for us a non-canonical psalm, but for the faithful at Qumrân it was seemingly as 'canonical' as Ps 144, which precedes it, or Ps 142, which follows it, in 11QPs[a]. (It should be noted that Gunkel calls Ps 144[1–11] a *Königsklagelied* and Ps 142 a *Klagepsalm eines Einzelnen*.) It was manifestly acceptable at Qumrân at the date of our scroll, but if it was known at Jamnia it was not acceptable to the Rabbis by the end of the first century A.D. Since there is no patent reason for the Rabbis to have rejected it, we should probably assume that it was not widely known and hence was not considered at Jamnia either Davidic or old enough to have come from the time of Ezra or before. At Qumrân it was clearly considered of

(1) Cf. the articles mentioned *supra*, p. 69, n. 1. Philonenko (p. 37) rightly insists that Syr No. I (LXX Ps 151) has nothing typically Essenian in it: *argumentum a fortiori* 11QPs 151.

(2) Cf. Paul Kahle, *The Cairo Geniza* (1959), pp. 17 ff. and 97 ff., and A. Di Lella, 'Qumrân and the Geniza Fragments of Sirach', *The Catholic Biblical Quarterly*, xxiv (1962), pp. 245–67.

Davidic origin; Cols. xxvii and xxviii of 11QPs^a establish quite clearly that the Qumrân psalter as a whole was attributed to David.(1)

Hence the Qumrânians certainly did not attribute Ps III or any other psalm in 11QPs^a to the Teacher of Righteousness. Ps II, which, as we have seen, may be of an early sectarian origin, likewise was not attributed to the Teacher, but, on the contrary, was venerated enough to be attributed to David and hence included in the Qumrân psalter. Ps III could very well be considerably older than Ps II. With Ps III we find ourselves in the same very weak position we are in when we try to solve the higher critical questions of date and authorship of the bulk of the canonical psalms. Perhaps the best we can hope to do with Pss II and III is to discern their uses in the cultic life of Qumrân.

Only a few conclusions can be drawn. (A) We now have in 11QPs^a the Hebrew 'Vorlagen' of the Syriac non-canonical Pss Nos. II and III. (B) Ps II is a sapiential hymn of possible proto-Essenian origin. (C) Ps III, by contrast, is quite 'biblical' in form and expression, being an individual *Danklied–Klagelied* combination, and like its canonical counterparts defies all facile attempts to assign it a date.

PLEA FOR DELIVERANCE

(11QPs^a Plea)

Col. XIX

COL. xix contains seventeen complete two-colon verses, and two three-colon verses, of an unknown psalm which may originally have had some twenty-four or twenty-five verses (perhaps five or six lines at the bottom of Col. xviii and another line or so at the bottom of Col. xix before the first line of Ps 139). Since the opening five or so verses are missing, it is difficult to determine what the stanza divisions may have been. The poem breaks naturally in l. 8, where שאגה נפשי begins an individual's *Danklied* for deliverance from death, followed in ll. 13 ff. by the psalmist's pleas for forgiveness of sin and deliverance from Satan.

The psalm is biblical in vocabulary, form, and content, and some verses are biblical paraphrases. The biblical argument that God should spare a man death since the dead cannot praise God is here repeated (Isa 38$^{18-19}$, Job 7^{21}, Ps 6$^{4-5}$, *et passim*). Ll. 14–16 remind one somewhat of 1QS iii and iv, but the vocabulary is different. שבחי of l. 16 is rabbinical (cf. Sirach 44^{1}). Here also are found Satan and the evil inclination of rabbinic literature rather than Belial and the spirit of wickedness of Qumrân, and the spirit of faithfulness rather than the spirit of truth.

Among the Cave 11 fragments assigned to Professor J. van der Ploeg and to be published by the Royal Dutch Academy are three which belong to another copy of our Plea for Deliverance. They offer a few words of a line preceding our first line and perhaps some evidence of a few words following our extant text. Otherwise the two texts are in close correspondence save for very few orthographic variants. Prof. van der Ploeg's text, however, does not seem to have been part of a scroll of biblical psalms.

Col. XIX
Lines

1 כי לוא רמה תודה לכה
ולוא תספר חסדכה תולעה
2 חי חי יודה לכה
יודו לכה כול מוטטי רגל

(1) Cf. the articles mentioned above, p. 69, n. 1.

Col. XIX
Lines

2–3 בהודיעכה חסדכה להמה
וצדקתכה תשכילם
3–4 כי בידכה נפש כול חי
נשמת כול בשר אתה נתתה
4–5 עשה עמנו יהוה כטובכה
כרוב רחמיכה
וכרוב צדקותיכה
5–6 שמע יהוה בקול אוהבי שמו
ולוא עזב חסדו מהמה
7–8 ברוך יהוה עושה צדקות
מעטר חסידיו חסד ורחמים
8–9 שאגה נפשי להלל את שמכה
להודות ברנה חסדיכה
9 להגיד אמונתכה
לתהלתכה אין חקר
9–10 למות הייתי בחטאי
ועוונותי לשאול מכרוני
10–11 ותצילני יהוה
כרוב רחמיכה
וכרוב צדקותיכה
11–12 גם אני את שמכה אהבתי
ובצלכה חסיתי
12–13 בזוכרי עוזכה יתקף לבי
ועל חסדיכה אני נסמכתי
13–14 סלחה יהוה לחטאתי
וטהרני מעווני
14–15 רוח אמונה ודעת חונני
אל אתקלה בעווה
15 אל תשלט בי שטן
ורוח טמאה
15–16 מכאוב ויצר רע
אל ירשו בעצמי
16–17 כי אתה יהוה שבחי
ולכה קויתי כול היום
17 ישמ͏̊חו אחי עמי
ובית אבי השוממים בחונכה
[ ]
18 [ ]לם אשמחה בכה

1. Surely a maggot cannot praise thee
   nor a grave-worm recount thy lovingkindness.

2. But the living can praise thee,
   (even) all those who stumble can laud thee.

2–3. In revealing thy kindness to them
   and by thy righteousness thou dost enlighten them.

3–4. For in thy hand is the soul of every living thing;
   the breath of all flesh hast thou given.

4–5. Deal with us, O Lord, according to thy goodness,
   according to thy great mercy,
   and according to thy many righteous deeds.

5–6. The Lord has heeded the voice of those who love his name
   and has not deprived them of his lovingkindness.

7–8. Blessed be the Lord, who executes righteous deeds,
   crowning his saints with lovingkindness and mercy.

8–9. My soul cries out to praise thy name,
   to sing high praises for thy loving deeds,

9. To proclaim thy faithfulness—
   of praise of thee there is no end.

9–10. Near death was I for my sins,
   and my iniquities had sold me to the grave;

10–11. But thou didst save me, O Lord,
   according to thy great mercy,
   and according to thy many righteous deeds.

11–12. Indeed have I loved thy name,
   and in thy protection have I found refuge.

12–13. When I remember thy might my heart is brave,
   and upon thy mercies do I lean.

13–14. Forgive my sin, O Lord,
   and purify me from my iniquity.

14–15. Vouchsafe me a spirit of faith and knowledge,
   and let me not be dishonoured in ruin.

15. Let not Satan rule over me,
   nor an unclean spirit;

15–16. Neither let pain nor the evil inclination
   take possession of my bones.

16–17. For thou, O Lord, art my praise,
   and in thee do I hope all the day.

17. Let my brothers rejoice with me
   and the house of my father, who are astonished by thy gracious . . .

18. [. . . . .]
   [For e]ver I will rejoice in thee.

L. 1: רמה. Cf. Isa 14^{11}, Job 17^{13} 24^{20}. The dead cannot praise God: cf. Isa 38^{18-19}, Ps 6^{4-5}, *et passim*.
L. 2: N.B.: The erasure of הוא following חי חי. Cf. Isa 38^{19}: חי חי הוא יודך.
Ll. 3–4: Cf. Job 12^{10}: אשר בידו נפש כל חי ורוח כל בשר איש. N.B.: The erasure of *he* before בשר.
Ll. 5–6: אוהבי שמו. Cf. Pss 5^{12} 69^{37} 119^{132}.
Ll. 7–8: מעטר וגו׳. Cf. Ps 103^{4}.
Ll. 8–9: N.B.: את is inserted above שמכה.
Ll. 9–10: חטאי. Parallel to עוונותי.
Ll. 12–13: נסמכתי. Cf. Ps 71^{6}.
Ll. 13–14: Cf. Ps 51^{4}, Jer 33^{8}, Numb 14^{9}.
חטאתי and עווני sing.
Ll. 14–15: רוח . . . חונני. Cf. 1QS ii 3 iv 4, 1QH iii 22–23.
עווה. Cf. Ezek 21^{32}. Read עויה (cf. Dan 4^{24})?

SIRACH $51^{13\text{ ff.}}$

(11QPs^a Sirach)

Col. XXI, ll. 11–17, Col. XXII, l. 1

COL. xxi, ll. 11–17, and Col. xxii, l. 1, contain the earliest Hebrew text to date of Sirach $51^{13-20b(?)}$ and 51^{30b}.

Until the recovery, in 1897, of the Cairo text of this portion of Ecclesiasticus, the canticle had been known only in Greek (Latin, Armenian, Slavonic, Ethiopic, Sahidic) and Syriac (Arabic).[(1)] The medieval text, from the Cairo Genizah, was published, with other fragments of Sirach, by S. Schechter and C. Taylor in 1899.[(2)]

H. L. Strack, Rudolf Smend, and others soon followed with their own considerations of the value and importance of the Cairo text.[(3)] G. Margoliouth, in his *The Origin of the 'Original Hebrew' of Ecclesiasticus*, in 1899, surmised that the Cairo text was a re-translation partly from the Syriac and partly from a Persian translation of the Greek. The negative aspect of his judgement now seems confirmed so far as the final canticle of Sirach is concerned.

G. Bickell, in 1882, had reconstructed from the versions an alphabetic arrangement of the canticle.[(4)] The Cairo text confirmed his judgement that the canticle was alphabetic and his reconstruction was seen to be generally sound.

However, the Cairo text presented grave uncertainties in the verses *'alef–lamed* both in the alphabetic sequence and in numerous readings. Taylor and Schechter cited the Cairo Sirach as 'manifestly corrupt' in places but especially in the canticle.[(5)] The Syr–Cairo text of the canticle is apparently better preserved beginning with the *mem* verse, but unfortunately only two words, the last two, of the second half of the poem are preserved in Q with which to compare the later manuscript from *mem* on.

The Q text leaves little doubt about its authenticity. It is clearly a valid first-century copy of the original composition, and not a reconstruction from the versions. There are only three words in the text which present serious difficulties and they are far from insurmountable (בתרה in v. 2, ועלה in v. 6, and טרתי in v. 9). It is regrettable, of course, that not more of the text is preserved, and it is unfortunate that a few words at the bottom of Col. xxi are less than certain. But where the text is clear it seems highly reliable.

(1) Swete's *The Old Testament in Greek*, ii (1891), and Lagarde's *Libri Veteris Testamenti Apocryphi Syriace* (1861).

(2) *The Wisdom of Ben Sira* (1899), hereinafter referred to as Taylor.

(3) Strack, *Die Sprüche Jesus', des Sohnes Sirachs* (1903). Smend, *Die Weisheit des Jesus Sirach*: Text (1906); *Index* (1907). M. Ṣ. Segal, ספר בן סירא (1953).

(4) *Zeitschrift für katholische Theologie*, vi (1882), pp. 326–30.

(5) p. lxxxvii.

The canticle is, as Bickell perceived and as the Cairo text indicated, an alphabetic acrostic. Where the Syr–Cairo text was the least secure in the alphabetic arrangement, the Q text supplies the sequence. The Q text, moreover, supplies a poem quite different from what Cairo and the versions offer.

The Greek is the closest to the text in Q, although not as close as the Cairo text is to the Syriac. The confusion exhibited among the Greek manuscripts (between B on the one hand and ℵ and A on the other) at Sirach vv. 19 and 20 receives some clarity now from Q if not full solution. Up to that point, however, Grk is parallel to Q in every stichos; i.e. Q now shows the order of Grk in vv. 13–18 to be correct and the order of Syr–Cairo corrupt. Both Bickell and those who later worked with the Cairo text anticipated the correctness of this observation.

Grk and Q, however, within the stichoi are so distinct both in form and content that close comparison of the two is imperative. The following transcriptions are set side by side in order to demonstrate the differences in the two texts. The distinctive elements in each are underscored; comparatively minor differences in syntax or meaning are overlooked.

	LXX (*apud* Swete)	Q	Col. XXI Lines
13	Ἔτι ὢν νεώτερος πρὶν ἢ πλανηθῆναί με	אני נער בטרם תעיתי	(1) 11
	ἐζήτησα σοφίαν προφανῶς ἐν προσευχῇ μου	ובקשתיה	
14	ἔναντι ναοῦ ἠξίουν περὶ αὐτῆς	באה לי בתרה	(2) 11–12
	καὶ ἕως ἐσχάτων ἐκζητήσω αὐτήν.	ועד סופה אדורשנה	
15a	ἐξ ἄνθους ὡς περκαζούσης σταφυλῆς	גם גרע נץ בבשול ענבים	(3) 12
	εὐφράνθη ἡ καρδία μου ἐν αὐτῇ	ישמחו לב	
15b	ἐπέβη ὁ πούς μου ἐν εὐθύτητι	דרכה רגלי במישור	(4) 13
	ἐκ νεότητός μου ἴχνευον αὐτήν.	כי מנעורי ידעתיה	
16	ἔκλινα ὀλίγον τὸ οὖς μου καὶ ἐδεξάμην	הטיתי כמעט אוזני	(5) 13–14
	καὶ πολλὴν εὗρον ἐμαυτῷ παιδείαν.	והרבה מצאתי לקח	
17	προκοπὴ ἐγένετό μοι ἐν αὐτῇ·	ועלה היתה לי	(6) 14–15
	τῷ διδόντι μοι σοφίαν δώσω δόξαν.	למלמדי אתן הודי	
18	διενοήθην γὰρ τοῦ ποιῆσαι αὐτήν	זמותי ואשחקה	(7) 15
	καὶ ἐζήλωσα τὸ ἀγαθόν	קנאתי בטוב	
	οὐ μὴ αἰσχυνθῶ.	ולוא אשוב	
19aα	διαμεμάχισται ἡ ψυχή μου ἐν αὐτῇ	חריתי נפשי בה	(8) 15–16
?		ופני לוא השיבותי	
20aα	τὴν ψυχήν μου κατεύθυνα εἰς αὐτήν	טרתי נפשי בה	(9) 16–17
		וברומיה לוא אשלה	
19bα	τὰς χεῖράς μου ἐξεπέτασα πρὸς ὕψος	ידי פתח[תי ...]	(10) 17
19bβ(?)	καὶ τὰ ἀγνοήματα αὐτῆς ἐπενόησα	[ו]מערמיה אתבונן	
		כפי הברותי אל ...	(11) 17

			Col. XXII Line
30b	(καὶ δώσει) τὸν μισθὸν ὑμῶν ἐν καιρῷ αὐτοῦ.	....] שכרכם בעתו	(23*b*) 1

The following translation of Q follows the stichotic arrangement above.

1. I was a young man before I had erred
   when I looked for her.
2. She came to me in her beauty
   when finally I sought her out.
3. Even (as) a blossom drops in the ripening of grapes,
   making glad the heart,
4. (So) my foot trod in uprightness;
   for from my young manhood have I known her.
5. I inclined my ear but a little
   and great was the persuasion I found.
6. And she became for me a nurse;
   to my teacher I give my ardour.
7. I purposed to make sport:
   I was zealous for pleasure,
   without pause.
8. I kindled my desire for her
   without distraction.
9. I bestirred my desire for her,
   and on her heights I do not waver.
10. I opened my hand(s) . . .
    and perceive her unseen parts.
11. I cleansed my hands . . .

A number of the words and phrases in the Hebrew are capable of more than one translation; these ambiguities are noted below. One suspects that the *mots à double entente* are intentional and that in those instances the two meanings were understood together.

Q v. 1 (Sirach 51^{13}):

בטרם תעיתי, so Grk. Bickell reconstructed לפני תעותי and Smend proposed בטרם תעיתי!

Q v. 2 (51^{14}):

Lacking in Syr and Cairo.

באה לי. Contrast Grk ἔναντι ναοῦ (באהלי ?).

בתרה, 'in her beauty'. For orthography cf. ותרו in 1QIs[b] 52^{14} and התור in 11QPs 151^{5b} (xxviii 9). Cf. Wisdom $7^{10,\,29}$ 8^{2}. An alternative reading בתרה 'in her searches' (F. M. Cross, Jr.) is possible; cf. Qoh 1^{13} 7^{25}.

ועד סופה. Cf. Qoh 3^{11} 12^{13}. 'Unto her depths'?

אדורשנה. Grk ἐκζητήσω. For orthography cf. iii 5 vi 12 xiv 5 xxiii 15. For sense cf. Qoh 1^{13}, I Chron 26^{31}, Ezek 20^{3}.

Q v. 3 (51^{15a}):

Lacking in Syr and Cairo.

גרע, 'drop, wither'. Cf. Jastrow, p. 271.

נץ בבשול ענבים. A literary conceit derived from Gen 40^{10} (not from Amos 9^{13} as suggested by Bickell). Figurative of the young man's reaching maturity and shedding the innocence of childhood.

ישמחו לב. Cf. Ps 104^{15}.

Q v. 4 (51^{15b}):

דרכה. Perhaps an attempt at continuing the figure of the ripening grapes by obliquely suggesting the pressing of grapes for wine.

רגלי. Euphemism?

במישור, 'in smoothness'. Grk ἐν εὐθύτητι. Cf. Cairo באמתה, and Smend's proposed באשרה. Bickell was correct. Cf. 1QH vii 25.

אדוני of Cairo and Syr is lacking in Q.

ידעתיה. Cf. Syr.

Q v. 5 (51[16]):

הטיתי כמעט אוזני. Lacking in Syr–Cairo? Bickell was correct. Grk καὶ ἐδεξάμην is lacking in Q.

לקח, 'seductive words'. Cf. Prv 7[21] and 16[21]. Grk παιδείαν, Cairo דעה, and Bickell מוסר all lack the literary ambiguity of Q!

Q v. 6 (51[17]):

ועָלָה, 'and a nurse', from עול (cf. I Sam 6[7, 10], Ps 78[71], Isa 40[11]). Here Wisdom is in the role of the nursing mother, parallel here to her role as the teacher of the young man. Here again, as in Q v. 3 above, the young man's reaching maturity and shedding the innocence of childhood are contracted in a phrase. In Sirach 15[2] Wisdom is called כאם וכאשת נעורים (Cairo). The figure of Wisdom as a youthful bride or mistress is not uncommon; see especially Prv 8[30] 9[1–6], Sirach 24[21], and Wisdom 7[12] 8[2]. Cf. also the figures in Isa 49[15] and Prv 5[18–19] (יעלת חן).

Strack's עֻלָּה (cf. Cairo v. 26, בעלה) was reasonable for the Cairo text, עלה היה, but does not fit the syntax of Q. Smend's assumption of the prefixed *waw* was correct. Grk προκοπή indicates a contrived וַעֲלָה, 'profit, advantage', but lacks support of context and parallelism.

לכבוד of Cairo (Syr) is lacking in Q and is extraneous. Added to complete the mistaken reading 'her yoke'?

הודי, 'my manhood'; cf. Prv 5[9] (Dan 10[8]). Cf. LXX[LUC].

Q v. 7 (51[18]):

זמותי. Cf. Prv 30[32] 31[16]. Smend's זממתי was essentially correct. With the following word a hendiadys or syndetic construction.

ואשחקה, 'make sport'. Cf. Prv 8[30], II Sam 6[5, 14 ff.]. For the *he* ending see above the section on orthography in the Introduction.

קנאתי. Grk ἐζήλωσα. Cf. Bickell's ואקנא.

בטוב, 'for pleasure'. Contrast all witnesses.

אשוב. Cf. Syr–Cairo אהפך. Cf. Grk αἰσχυνθῶ (אבוש).

Q v. 8 (51[19]):

חריתי נפשי, 'I kindled my desire'. Cf. Grk διαμεμάχηται, 'strove' (cf. חרה in Jer 12[5] 22[15]). Cf. Syr ܐܬܚܡܬ, and Cairo חשקה. Taylor's attempt to wrest a *ṭet* verse from this line was ingenious. It is now clear that all the witnesses purged the text of its sensuous overtones; hence the erotic חריתי נפשי בה became Syr–Cairo חשקה נפשי בה, the Grk notion of striving and the Lat that of the troubled soul (*colluctata est anima mea*). V. 8*b* (> LXX) is in Syr.

Q v. 9 (Grk v. 20*a*, Lat v. 27*a* (?)):

Only Syr–Cairo has this verse in its proper place. Taylor, Smend, Charles, *et al.* construct a *kaf* verse corresponding to Grk–Lat.

טרתי. Grk κατεύθυνα strongly suggests טרדתי (> *ṭāratti*, cf. Sirach 32[9]), in transitive force, 'to carry, banish, stir up, trouble, agitate' (Jastrow, p. 550), chiastically parallel to לוא אשלה and complementary to חריתי (v. 8). Taylor (p. lxxxii) suggested טרדה for the *ṭet* verse but forcedly tried to relate it to Syr–Cairo חשקה, which, on the contrary, represents Q v. 8 (Grk v. 19).

וברומיה, 'and in her heights'. Cf. Wisdom on the heights in Prv 8[2] 9[3, 14]. Cf. Ezek 16[24, 25].

לוא אשלה, 'I do not relax'. Cf. II Chron 29[11] and οὐ μὴ ἐγκαταλειφθῶ in Grk v. 20.

Q v. 10 (Grk v. 19*b*, Lat v. 26, Syr v. 20*c*):

ידי. Euphemism?

פתח[ת]י. With Grk ἐξεπέτασα (Syr–Cairo has פתחה). Cf. Cant 5[4–5] and Assyrian *patâḫu*, 'penetrate, bore'.

מַעֲרֻמֶּיהָ, 'her nakedness'. Cf. II Chron 28[15]. מֵעֲרֻמֶּיהָ (cf. Sirach 42[18] (?), Job 5[12]) or מֵעָרְמִיה (cf. Job 5[13]), 'from her shrewdness I gain understanding', are possible readings though not probable. Grk τὰ ἀγνοήματα αὐτῆς, 'the unknown things about her', is a reasonable understanding of מַעֲרֻמֶּיהָ (so Skehan).

אתבונן, 'I consider carefully' ('pierce'?). For same sense and syntax cf. Job 30[20], Jer 30[24]; cf. Cairo . . . ואביט ב and Syr v. 20*c*, with Segal *et al.* Grk ἐπένθησα is an error for ἐπενόησα = אתבונן.

Q v. 11*a* is lacking in all the witnesses.
Sirach 51^{30}, 11QPs^a xxii 1:
שכרכם בעתו. So all the witnesses.

There can be little doubt that Grk presents an interpretive recension of the canticle. While Q may possibly not represent the original text of the poem in all details, it is clearly superior to Syr–Cairo and Lat. And while it does not appear at first blush to be superior to Grk, it is none the less the text which must now receive priority. The answers to the problems raised by the acrostic sequence of the canticle are found not in Grk, but in Q (cf. Bickell) and certainly not in the Syr–Cairo tradition. But, more importantly, it is now quite clear that the canticle is totally independent of Sirach. If Jesus, son of Sira, of Jerusalem, had penned the canticle it would hardly be found in 11QPs^a, which claims Davidic authorship. That neither David nor Ben Sira wrote it needs no comment. What is interesting, of course, is that in Palestine it could be considered Davidic while contemporarily in Alexandria it became related to the later 'Jerusalem' sage.

Internal comparisons between Q and Grk illustrate the original independence of the poem. The first and most obvious observation is that *πρὶν ἢ πλανηθῆναί με* is a good translation of בטרם תעיתי; but attached to Ben Sira it lost its primitive significance, that of erring, and took on the foreign connotation of reference to Ben Sira's travels (39^4).[1] In the same verse, and the following, the Grk interjects a theme of cultic piety and prayer quite foreign to Q, but integral to the themes in Sirach, which probably originally ended with praise of Simon, the high priest, son of Onias (50^{1-24}). Where the Grk says, 'Before the temple I asked for her', Q says, 'She came to me in her beauty' (Grk v. 14, Q v. 2). Where Grk suggests that Ben Sira had followed in Wisdom's footsteps from his youth, Q says the poet had intimate knowledge of Wisdom (Grk v. 15*b*, Q v. 3—cf. Syr). Where Grk speaks of Ben Sira's receiving Wisdom (Cairo, 'learning Wisdom'), Q is silent (Grk v. 16*a*). Where Grk speaks of the sage's finding much instruction, Q uses the more ambiguous and pregnant לקח (Grk v. 16*b*, Q v. 5*b*).

It is at Grk v. 17 that the marked differences begin to occur. Where Grk speaks of the sage's profiting by Wisdom, Q speaks of Wisdom's being a nurse (Grk v. 17*a*, Q v. 6*a*); and where Grk speaks of rendering glory to God, Q speaks of dedicating his vigour to his teacher, manifestly Wisdom herself (Grk v. 17*b*, Q v. 6*a*)! Grk substitutes in v. 18 the notion of acting according to Wisdom for the Q idea of making sport; Grk then makes of the Q statement of zeal for pleasure the innocuous zeal for good (Grk v. 18, Q v. 7). In Q vv. 8–9 the ideas of kindling and directing the desire (נפשי) become in Grk that of the troubled but determined soul. The closing phrases of Q vv. 7–9, which present a picture of youthful concentration on an object of passion, are muted in Grk. The Q idea of not relaxing in Wisdom's heights (v. 9) is modified in Grk to that of being strict of conduct ($51^{19a\beta}$).

One can only conjecture what may have been the full statements of the *kaf* and *lamed* verses. The former is omitted entirely from Syr–Cairo, Grk, and Lat. And while it may conceivably lie latent among the confused elements of 51^{20} in the various witnesses, extreme caution is in order because of the absence in them of anything corresponding to Q . . . כפי הברותי אל. *Lamed*, on the contrary, may well have been a statement about the לב as noted in Syr–Cairo, Grk, and Lat. The *mem* verse in Syr–Cairo commends itself as highly authentic: 'My loins are astir like a firepot for her, to gaze upon her, that I may own her, a pleasant possession.' It is overloaded as it stands, but it clearly follows the thought sequence of extant Q and stands over against Grk v. 21 in the manner of Q's distinction from Grk elsewhere.

(1) Cf. Taylor, p. lxxx, Smend, p. 495, and R. H. Charles, *Apocrypha and Pseudepigrapha*, i (1913), *ad loc.*

LXX[B]	Cairo
καὶ ἡ κοιλία μου ἐταράχθη ἐκζητῆσαι αὐτήν *διὰ τοῦτο ἐκτησάμην ἀγαθὸν κτῆμα.*	מעי יהמו כתנור לה להביט בה בעבור כן קניתיה קנין טוב

It is undeniable that beginning with *mem* (51^{21}) Syr–Cairo inspires the confidence lacking in the earlier lines. The alphabetic sequence is in full evidence in Cairo, save for the *samekh* and *shin* verses, where Syr affords the obvious solutions. But, more importantly, Syr–Cairo vv. 21–30 (*mem* ff.) stands in about the same relation to Grk–Lat as does Q up to v. 19. It is not surprising that the differences are not as striking among the extant witnesses for the latter part of the canticle as for the first part. The first part of the poem is the Wisdom teacher's confession of his youthful experience with Wisdom as his nurse, teacher, and mistress, a commendable manner of sublimation in celibacy and undoubtedly highly meaningful in every spiritual sense for the celibates at Qumrân. But the second part of the canticle could hardly be offensive to the most delicate sensibility. It is concerned principally with an exhortation on the part of the teacher to current and prospective students to follow his example. He pleads in closing, 'And be not ashamed of my song' (Syr–Cairo; cf. LXX). It is possible that the *qof*, *resh*, and *shin* verses in Syr–Cairo may represent some purposive tampering with the original text, but otherwise from *mem* to the end Syr–Cairo seems highly reliable.[(1)] Margoliouth's thesis that the Cairo text is a retranslation may be true, but there is surely high authenticity in the latter half of the Syr–Cairo tradition.[(2)]

Syr–Cairo represents one tradition of transmission and Grk–Lat another.[(3)] Grk, however, is an internally consistent interpretive rendering, displaying throughout the same consistent relationship to the whole poem, to extant Q in the first part and to Syr–Cairo in the latter. Syr–Cairo, by contrast, while representing a disrupted recension of the first part of the poem, reflects a highly authentic rendering from *mem* to the end.

Our canticle is of the genre represented by the hymns of praise to Wisdom in Wisdom of Solomon $8^{2 \text{ ff.}}$ and Sirach $15^{1 \text{ ff.}}$, where Wisdom is desired as a bride of youth (*γυνὴ παρθενείας*—cf. Prv 5^{18}). The mixing of the figure of the bride with that of a nurse, or a mother giving suck (Q v. 6), is already familiar in Sirach 15^{2-3} (Grk and Cairo; cf. Sirach 24^{19-22}). The mixed metaphor suggests the further figure of Wisdom as a young man's mistress. In Prv 9^{1-6} Wisdom's maids call to men, from the high places of the town (cf. Q v. 9: cf. Prv 8^{2}), to turn into Wisdom's house to eat of her bread and drink of her wine. Wisdom's allurement is then contrasted with the harlot who calls, from the high places of the town, to men to turn into her house; but the harlot's water is stolen water and her bread must be eaten in secret (Prv 9^{13-18}). Wisdom is a fitting mistress for a young man even after she has been his nursing mother in his childhood.[4]

Our song tells of the experience of a young man who, at the stage in life when he was maturing from childhood into manhood (when as the blossom drops in the maturing of grapes, before he had yet erred), took Wisdom, who had been his nurse and continued to be his teacher, as his mistress. He dedicated his normally developing passions and desires to the pleasures of life with Wisdom, and he did so unstintingly, without pause, without distraction, and without respite.

The origin of the canticle is obscure. It is as Palestinian as Proverbs and Ecclesiastes (and

(1) Syr ܣܘܪܘ (סורו) for *samekh* is undoubtedly correct.

(2) There are indications that Cairo is not a translation of Syr exclusively in the latter part of the song. Cf. Nestle in his article on Sirach in Hastings, *Dictionary of the Bible*, iv, pp. 547 f.

(3) The relation of Lat to Grk is problematic. Cf. Charles, *op. cit.* i, pp. 289 f.

(4) Cf. H. Ringgren, *Word and Wisdom* (1947), pp. 111 ff.

Wisdom?). If the witnesses offer us an accurate reflection of the latter half of the poem it was indeed probably a song composed by a Wisdom teacher as a plea to his students to gain Wisdom from him and to espouse her as he had done in his youth. If so, it fits the context of Sirach better than the context of a Davidic psalter. But at Qumrân it was clearly thought to be one of the 450 songs (xxvii 10) which David composed.[(1)]

Several inferences may be drawn. (1) 11QPS^a contains a highly authentic text, if not the original text, of the canticle in Sirach $51^{13-ca. 20}$, and the last two words of v. 30. (2) 11QPs^a proves that the canticle was originally independent of Sirach and adapted to the latter only at great expense to the original poem. (3) It is a Wisdom teacher's song of his experience of intimate knowledge of Wisdom in his youth. The experience is related in muted but distinctly erotic tones. (4) It shows the early versions (Grk–Lat, Syr) to be partially interpretive translations, relying perhaps on intermediate recensions. In this regard it serves for the Sirach canticle the same purpose 11QPs 151 serves for LXX (Syr and Lat) Ps 151. (5) Schechter's Cairo Genizah text is probably, as suggested by G. Margoliouth in 1899, a retranslation. Margoliouth's thesis, however, should now be limited to two specifics: to apply only to the Syr–Cairo tradition as opposed to the Grk; and to apply probably only to the first part (*'alef* to *lamed*) of the canticle. (6) Applied to David, the canticle, like 11QPs 151, gives further insight into Jewish views in Hellenistic-Roman times of David's youth. (7) And, like 11QPs 151, it calls for renewed intensive examination of the early history of the hagiographic and apocryphal LXX.

APOSTROPHE TO ZION

(11QPs^a Zion)

Col. XXII, ll. 1–15

COL. xxii, ll. 1–15, contains, in its entirety, an apostrophe to Zion in the style of those familiar in Isa 54^{1-8} 60^{1-22} and 62^{1-8}. Isa 62^{6-8} speaks of those who put Yahweh in remembrance of his promises to Zion; the poet of our apostrophe is such a one. The apostrophe is to Zion, not to God, and hence is not a promethean prayer in itself. See the recent study by Brevard Childs, *Memory and Tradition in Israel* (1962), especially pp. 36–37 and 41 ff. (cf. xvii 17).

Much of the vocabulary and imagery is taken from the book of Isaiah, and especially Isa 66^{10-11}, as may be seen from a cursory perusal of the apparatus. Vv. 1 and 15 set the theme: Zion is in the prayers of all those who love her; and in those prayers God is reminded of the promises of the prophets toward her (vv. 6 and 17).

The metre is principally the double-colon 3/3, with four exceptions: vv. 1 and 18 are 3/3/3, and vv. 2 and 7 3/4.

The poem is an irregular alphabetic acrostic. There appear to be two *bet* colons, on the one hand, and a syncope of colons between *he* and *zayin* and between *resh* and *taw*, on the other hand. If we allow for the irregularities, symmetry emerges if sixteen bi-colons (*gimel* through *qof*) are seen as introduced and concluded by initial and closing tri-colons, yielding a poem of eighteen verses in all.

The vocabulary is essentially biblical though there are a few neo-Hebrew forms and a few very rare if not unique forms (see apparatus).

(1) Cf. xxvii 2, where it is said, ויהי דויד בן ישי חכם.

		Verse No.		Col. XXII Lines
	אזכירך לברכה ציון	(1)	א	1–2
	בכול מודי אני אהבתיך		ב	
3/3/3	ברוך לעולמים זכרך			
	גדולה תקותך ציון	(2)	ג	2–3
3/4	ושלום ותוחלת ישועתך לבוא			
	דור ודור ידורו בך	(3)	ד	3–4
3/3	ודורות חסידים תפארתך			
	המתאוים ליום ישעך	(4)	ה	4
3/3	וישישו ברוב כבודך		ו	
	זיז כבודך יינקו	(5)	ז	4–5
3/3	וברחובות תפארתך יעכסו			
	חסדי נביאיך תזכורי	(6)	ח	5–6
3/3	ובמעשי חסידיך תתפארי			
	טהר חמס מגוך	(7)	ט	6–7
3/4	שקר ועול נכרתו ממך			
	יגילו בניך בקרבך	(8)	י	7
3/3	וידידיך אליך נלוו			
	כמה קוו לישועתך	(9)	כ	8
3/3	ויתאבלו עליך תמיך			
	לוא תובד תקותך ציון	(10)	ל	8–9
3/3	ולוא תשכח תוחלתך			
	מי זה אבד צדק	(11)	מ	9–10
3/3	או מי זה מלט בעולו			
	נבחן אדם כדרכו	(12)	נ	10
3/3	איש כמעשיו ישתלם			
	סביב נכרתו צריך ציון	(13)	ס	10–11
3/3	ויתפזרו כול משנאיך			
	ערבה באף תשבחתך ציון	(14)	ע	11–12
3/3	מעלה לכול תבל			
	פעמים רבות אזכירך לברכה	(15)	פ	12
3/3	בכול לבבי אברכך			
	צדק עולמים תשיגי	(16)	צ	13
3/3	וברכות נכבדים תקבלי			

			Verse No.	Col. XXII Lines
	קחי חזון דובר עליך	ק	(17)	13–14
3/3	וחלמות נביאים תתבעך			
	רומי ורחבי ציון	ר	(18)	14–15
	שבחי עליון פודך	ש		
3/3/3	תשמח נפשי בכבודך	ת		

1. I remember thee for blessing, O Zion;
   with all my might have I loved thee.
   May thy memory be blessed for ever!
2. Great is thy hope, O Zion:
   that peace and thy longed-for salvation will come.
3. Generation after generation will dwell in thee
   and generations of saints will be thy splendour:
4. Those who yearn for the day of thy salvation
   that they may rejoice in the greatness of thy glory.
5. On (the) abundance of thy glory they are nourished
   and in thy splendid squares will they toddle.
6. The merits of thy prophets wilt thou remember,
   and in the deeds of thy pious ones wilt thou glory.

7. Purge violence from thy midst;
   falsehood and evil will be cut off from thee.
8. Thy sons will rejoice in thy midst
   and thy precious ones will be united with thee.
9. How they have hoped for thy salvation,
   thy pure ones have mourned for thee.
10. Hope for thee does not perish, O Zion,
    nor is hope in thee forgotten.
11. Who has ever perished (in) righteousness,
    or who has ever survived in his iniquity?
12. Man is tested according to his way;
    every man is requited according to his deeds;
13. All about are thine enemies cut off, O Zion,
    and all thy foes have been scattered.

14. Praise from thee is pleasing to God, O Zion,
    ascending through all the world.
15. Many times do I remember thee for blessing;
    with all my heart I bless thee.
16. Mayst thou attain unto everlasting righteousness,
    and blessings of the honourable mayst thou receive.

17. Accept a vision bespoken of thee,
and dreams of prophets sought for thee.
18. Be exalted, and spread wide, O Zion;
praise the Most High, thy saviour:
let my soul be glad in thy glory.

V. 1 (ll. 1–2):

אזכירך, 'I cause thee to be remembered', cf. Isa 62[6–7], those who remind Yahweh of Jerusalem until he will make of her a praise in the land. Forgetting Jerusalem (v. 10) would be failure to pray for her (Ps 137[5–6]): cf. *infra* v. 15, and Childs, *op. cit.*, p. 64.

מודי, for מאודי. For orthography cf. תובד for תואבד in v. 10, התור for התואר in xxviii 8, מודה for מואדה in 1QS x 16, &c. For sense cf. Deut 6[5], II Kings 23[25].

אהבתיך. Cf. Isa 66[10] (Pss 78[68] 87[2] 122[6]).

V. 3 (l. 4):

תפארתך. Cf. Isa 60[19] 62[3].

V. 4 (l. 4):

המתאוים. Cf. Ps 132[13–14].

וישישו. Cf. Isa 66[10] (65[18–19]).

V. 5 (ll. 4–5):

זיו כבודך. Cf. Isa 66[11], מזיו כבודך. N.B.: The space before זיו.

יינקו. Cf. Isa 66[11].

יעכסו, 'rattle bangles' (Isa 3[16–18]), from Arabic عَكَّسَ, 'hopple', hence 'tottle' or 'toddle', from the parallel figure of the child nursing.

V. 6 (ll. 5–6):

חסדי, 'pious deeds' (II Chron 32[32] 35[26]). One thinks as well of the חסדי דויד of Isa 55[3] and II Chron 6[42], perhaps here meaning God's promises of hope and restoration for Jerusalem given through the prophets. Cf. Isa 63[7], חסדי יהוה אזכיר.

V. 7 (ll. 6–7):

טהר (?). Infinitive with imperative force? Or read טהרי? Or טַהֵר?

מגוך. Cf. Isa 51[23].

ועול. If it were the *nomen opificum* it would probably be עוול, cf. בעולו *infra* v. 11.

V. 8 (l. 7):

יגילו וגו׳. Cf. Isa 66[10] 65[18–19]. N.B.: The space after יגילו, due to poor skin surface.

V. 9 (l. 8):

ויתאבלו. Cf. Isa 66[10].

תֻּמַּיִךְ. Cf. תמימים in xviii 1, 1QS iii 3 *et passim*; 1QM xiv 7, 1QH i 36, &c. Cf. also Ps 37[18], Prv 2[21], &c.

V. 10 (ll. 8–9):

תובד, for תואבד. For orthography cf. *supra* note to v. 1.

V. 11 (ll. 9–10):

מלט. Qal usage unique in Hebrew to my knowledge. Jastrow does not list מְלַט in rabbinic usage (בלט and נמלט are both unlikely). The sense of 'survive' (cf. Accadian *balâṭu*, 'to be healthy, alive') is indicated. Cf. Ps 37[25] and Isa 57[1].

V. 12 (l. 10):

נבחן. Rare, but clear here.

איש. N.B.: Erasure of *nun* of אנוש (?).

ישתלם. Derived from Aramaic ithpeʿil? N.B.: Erasure of *he* after ישתלם.

V. 13 (ll. 10–11):
ויתפזרו. Rare in Tannaitic literature.

V. 14 (ll. 11–12):
עָרְבָה באף, 'sweet to the nose', used of sacrifices in MT: cf. Mal 3^{4}.
תֻּשבָּחתך. Tannaitic and rabbinic. Zion's praise of God (cf. v. 18).
מעֹלה באף. Noun? Adverb?

V. 15 (l. 12):
Cf. *supra* v. 1.

V. 16 (l. 13):
צדק עולמים. Cf. this and the next verse with Dan 9^{24}.

V. 17 (ll. 13–14):
דּוּבַּר. Rare. With נכבדים of v. 16, cf. Ps 87^{3}, נכבדות מדבר בך, also in reference to Zion. Note the lack of אשר.
תתבעך. יִתְבָּעֶךְ (?), from בעה (cf. Isa 21^{12}) with dative suffix of reference. From תבע?

V. 18 (ll. 14–15):
רומי. Cf. Prv 11^{11}, בברכת ישרים תרום קרת. Cf. קומי in Isa 51^{17} 52^{2} 60^{1}, Micah 4^{13}.
ורחבי. Cf. הרחיבי in Isa 54^{2}.
שבחי. Cf. Ps 147^{12}.

HYMN TO THE CREATOR

(11QPs^{a} Creat.)

Col. XXVI, ll. 9–15

IN Col. xxvi, ll. 9–15, are nine verses of a sapiential hymn of praise to the Creator. It has vague affinities with the *Hodayot* (see notes) in the first six verses, but vv. 7–9 are made up of phrases which are found in Jer 10^{12-13} (51^{15-16}) and Ps 135^{7}.

The metre is highly irregular and the language is forced and pedestrian. The imagery and vocabulary are late, in biblical terms.

The phrases in vv. 7–9 appear in better order here than in Jeremiah or Ps 135. The three colons of Q vv. 8*b*–9 are in reverse order in the biblical passages; and Jer $10^{13a\alpha}$ is lacking in Q. This material undoubtedly derives from some liturgical hymn of praise of the Creator. While it is highly possible that our psalm in 11QPs^{a} represents an authentic text of the original sapiential hymn from which the material in Jeremiah was derived, caution is in order in dealing with Ps 135, which lacks any explicit reference to Wisdom and is probably earlier than the Q psalm.

	Verse No.	Col. XXVI Lines
גדול וקדוש יהוה	(1)	9
קדוש קדושים לדור ודור		
לפניו הדר ילך	(2)	9–10
ואחריו המון מים רבים		
חסד ואמת סביב פניו	(3)	10–11
אמת ומשפט וצדק מכון כסאו		
מבדיל אור מאפלה	(4)	11–12
שחר הכין בדעת לבו		

	Verse No.	Col. XXVI Lines
אז ראו כול מלאכיו וירננו	(5)	12
כי הראם את אשר לוא ידעו		
מעטר הרים תנובות	(6)	13
אוכל טוב לכול חי		
ברוך עושה ארץ בכוחו	(7)	13–14
מכין תבל בחוכמתו		
בתבונתו נטה שמים	(8)	14–15
ויוצא [רוח] מאו[צרותיו]		
[ברקים למט]ר עשה	(9)	15
ויעל נ̊שיא̊[ים מ]ק̊צ̊ה [ארץ]		

1. Great and holy is the Lord,
   the holiest unto every generation.
2. Majesty precedes him,
   and following him is the rush of many waters.
3. Grace and truth surround his presence;
   truth and justice and righteousness are
   the foundation of his throne.
4. Separating light from deep darkness,
   by the knowledge of his mind he
   established the dawn.
5. When all his angels had witnessed it they sang aloud,
   for he showed them what they had not known:
6. Crowning the hills with fruit,
   good food for every living being.
7. Blessed be he who makes the earth by his power,
   establishing the world in his wisdom.
8. By his understanding he stretched out the heavens,
   and brought forth [wind] from his st[orehouses].
9. He made [lightning for the rai]n,
   and caused mist[s] to rise [from] the end of [the earth].

V. 1 (l. 9):
קדוש קדושים. Cf. Ps 89^{6-8}, Hos 12^{1}, Zech 14^{5}, 1QH iii 22, 35 *et passim* in Q literature; cf. מלך מלכים in Tannaitic idiom.

V. 2 (ll. 9–10):
המון מים רבים. Cf. Jer 10^{13aa} (51^{16aa}) 51^{13}, 1QH ii 16.

V. 3 (ll. 10–11):
מכון כסאו. Cf. Pss 85^{11} 89^{15} 97^{2}.

V. 4 (ll. 11–12):
שחר הכין. Cf. Hos 6^{3}, 1QH iv 6.
בדעת לבו. Cf. 1QS x 24. Rare if not unique in reference to God.

V. 5 (l. 12):

אזראו. Read אז ראו. For grammatical construction cf. Ps 89^{20}.

כי הראם את אשר לוא ידעו. Cf. [ידעו] כי הראיתם את אשר לא in 1QH xiii 11. N.B.: Erasure of *he* (?) before הראם.

V. 6 (l. 13):

N.B.: Erasure of *waw* and blank space before אוכל.

Vv. 7–9 (ll. 13–15):

See Jer $10^{12,\ 13b\beta,\ 13b\alpha,\ 13a\beta}$ $51^{15,\ 16b\beta,\ 16b\alpha,\ 16a\beta}$. Cf. Ps 135^{7} (xiv 15). Jer 10^{12-13}:

עשה ארץ בכחו מכין תבל בחכמתו ובתבונתו נטה שמים
לקול תתו המון מים בשמים ויעלה נשאים מקצה ארץ
ברקים למטר עשה ויוצא רוח מאצרתיו

ברוך is peculiar to Q. LXX has κύριος in Jer 10^{12} but not in 51^{15}. לקול תתו > LXX Jer 10^{13}.

Read רוח in v. 8*b* with MT Jer 10^{13}. אור (φῶς) of LXX^{B} Jer 10^{13} (28^{16}) is possible, but רוחות of the other witnesses and of LXX Ps 135^{7} (ἀνέμους) does not fit the lacuna. Some LXX mss read מאצרתיה.

DAVID'S COMPOSITIONS

(11QPs^{a} DavComp)

Col. XXVII, ll. 2–11

THE only prose composition in the scroll (with the possible exception of the subscription to Ps 145 in xvii 17 f.) is found in Col. xxvii, ll. 2–11. It states that David wrote not only psalms but also 'songs'. Of the former he composed 3,600, and of the latter, 450. Concerning the psalms only the number is given (l. 5), but concerning the songs both the type of song and the number of each type are given:

For the daily *ʿolat hat-tamid* (l. 6)	364
For the Sabbath *qorban* (l. 7)	52
For the *qorban* of the New Moons, Solemn Assemblies, and the Day of Atonement (l. 8)	30
Total (l. 9)	446
'Songs for the Stricken' (l. 10)	4
Psalms (l. 5)	3,600
Grand Total (l. 10)	4,050

The listing for the *qorban* and *tamid* offerings will evoke considerable interest in the light of the Enoch–Jubilees–Qumrân 364-day, 52-Sabbath year.[1] The distinction between psalm and song and the latter's application to cultic usage will evoke considerable form-critical interest.

[1] Cf. A. Jaubert, 'Le Calendrier des Jubilés et de la secte de Qumrân', *Vetus Testamentum*, iii (1953), pp. 250–64; S. Talmon, 'The Calendar Reckoning of the Sect from the Judaean Desert', in *Aspects of the Dead Sea Scrolls* (*Scripta Hierosolymitana*, iv) (1958), pp. 162–99; J. M. Baumgarten in *Journal of Biblical Literature*, lxxvii (1958), pp. 249–57 and 355–60; and Talmon in *Revue de Qumrân*, viii (1960), pp. 475–500. On the psalms for the *tamid* offering and especially for the Sabbath day cf. N. Sarna, *Journal of Biblical Literature*, lxxvi (1962), pp. 155–68. See also M. Baillet, *Revue biblique*, lxviii (1961), pp. 212 and 233, in reference to l. 7 below (הודות ביום השבת, 4QBt 3: vii: 4 ff.); and J. Strugnell, Supplements to *Vetus Testamentum*, vii (1959), pp. 318–45 (4QS 37–39).

The literary activity here ascribed to David seems to challenge Solomon's record as noted in I Kings 5^{12}. There it is said that Solomon wrote proverbs and songs and here it is said that David wrote psalms and songs. 1,005 songs are claimed for Solomon and 450 for David; 3,000 proverbs are claimed for Solomon and 3,600 psalms for David. They both wrote 'songs': it is the number of Solomon's songs that varies in the versions;[1] and it is the 'song' that has the cultic reference here (cf. II Sam 22 (Ps $18)^{1}$, Amos 6^{5}, I Chron 6^{16} 16^{7-42} 25^{7}, II Chron 7^{6} 29^{26-30}).

David is credited with the divine gift of prophecy (l. 11) in composing his psalms and songs. Several of the attributes of David listed in ll. 2–4 are found in II Sam 23^{1-7}, which immediately precedes in Cols. xxvi and xxvii, l. 1, or in II Sam 22 (Ps 18), which was surely included in the early columns of 11QPs[a] (see notes).

David's attributes of wisdom reflect the speech of the wise woman of Tekoa to David in II Sam 14^{20}, the paragraph in I Sam 16^{12b-23}, and the expressions in II Sam 23^{4}. David's being called *ḥakham* is interesting in the light of the apocryphal sapiential psalms included in the scroll (Cols. xviii, xxi, and xxvi). Especially interesting is the inclusion in the scroll of the variant Hebrew text of Sirach $51^{13\text{ ff.}}$ (Col. xxi). The last three columns of 11QPs[a] clearly state a claim for the Davidic authorship of the Psalter as represented by the scroll, the earliest literary evidence of belief in the Davidic authorship of the Psalter (see the section on Ps 151). At Qumrân David was thought of not only as a musical composer and author of the Psalter under prophetic inspiration, but also as a *ḥakham*, capable of the kind of thinking elsewhere attributed to the great Wisdom teacher Ben Sira.

Col. XXVII
Lines

2 ויהי דויד בן ישי חכם ואור כאור השמש וסופר
3 ונבון ותמים בכול דרכיו לפני אל ואנשים ויתן
4 לו י ה ו ה רוח נבונה ואורה ויכתוב תהלים
5 שלושת אלפים ושש מאות ושיר לשורר לפני המזבח על עולת
6 התמיד לכול יום ויום לכול ימי השנה ארבעה וששים ושלוש
7 מאות ולקורבן השבתות שנים וחמשים שיר ולקורבן ראשי
8 החודשים ולכול ימי המועדות ולים הכפורים שלושים שיר
9 ויהי כול השיר אשר דבר ששה ואבעים וארבע מאות ושיר
10 לנגן על הפגועים ארבעה ויהי הכול ארבעת אלפים וחמשים
11 כול אלה דבר בנבואה אשר נתן לו מלפני העליון

2. And David, the son of Jesse, was wise, and a light like the light of the sun, and literate,
3. and discerning and perfect in all his ways before God and men. And the Lord gave
4. him a discerning and enlightened spirit. And he wrote
5. 3,600 psalms; and songs to sing before the altar over the whole-burnt
6. *tamid* offering every day, for all the days of the year, 364;
7. and for the *qorban* of the Sabbaths, 52 songs; and for the *qorban* of the New
8. Moons and for all the Solemn Assemblies and for the Day of Atonement, 30 songs.
9. And all the songs that he spoke were 446, and songs
10. for making music over the stricken, 4. And the total was 4,050.
11. All these he spoke through prophecy which was given him from before the Most High.

(1) 5,000 songs in the versions; cf. LXX III Kings 4^{32}.

Ll. 2–4: The first three lines are indented three centimetres because of rough skin surface (scar tissue?) in the leather (see 'Surface Observations' in the Introduction).

L. 2: **חכם**. Cf. the speech of the wise woman of Tekoa to David in II Sam 14^{20}.
ואור כאור השמש. Cf. **וכאור בקר יזרח שמש** in reference to David in II Sam 23^{4}, which would have appeared only a few lines earlier in the previous column.
וסופר. The first *waw* is inserted above the *samekh*. 'Literate' or 'scholarly'; cf. I Chron 27^{32}, TB *Berakhot* 45*b*.

L. 3: **ונבון**. Cf. **ונבון דבר** in reference to David in I Sam 16^{18}, and **לב חכם ונבון** in reference to Solomon in I Kings 3^{12}.
ותמים. Cf. **תמים** in reference to David in Ps 18 (II Sam 22)$^{24, 26, 33}$. The phrase **ויתן (ויתר) תמים דרכי** in v. 33 perhaps gave rise to **ותמים בכול דרכיו** here.

L. 4: **רוח נבונה ואורה**. Cf. **רוח יהוה דבר בי** in II Sam 23^{2}, and the paragraph on the divine spirit and David's musical abilities in I Sam 16^{12b-23} (especially **נבון דבר** in v. 18). Cf. also Isa 11^{2}.

L. 5: Cf. **שיר** and the instruments of 'song' in reference to David: II Sam 22 (Ps 18)^{1}, Amos 6^{5}, I Chron 6^{16} 16$^{7-42}$ 25^{7}, II Chron 7^{6} 29$^{26-30}$.

Ll. 6–7: Mishnah *Tamid* 7^{4} lists Pss 24, 48, 82, 94, 81, 93, and 92 for levitical singing on the seven days of the week. Cf. the superscriptions to LXX Pss 23 (first day), 47 (second), 93 (fourth), 92 (sixth), and 91 (Sabbath).

L. 8: **ולים**. There is space available for the omitted *waw*!

L. 9: **ואבעים**. Read **וארבעים**.

L. 10: **הפגועים**. Cf. **שיר הפגועים** (Ps 91) in TJ *Erubin* x. 26*c*; TJ *Shabbat* vi. 8*b*; and *Midrash Tehillim* to Ps 91 (Jastrow, p. 1135), the song of demons or of evil spirits or for the stricken.

L. 11: **בנבואה**. Cf. II Chron 9^{29} 15^{8}, Neh 6^{12}.

INDEX OF HEBREW WORDS IN THE APOCRYPHALS

אבי: xix 17 xxviii 3
אבד: xxii 9
תובד: xxii 8
ויתאבלו: xxii 8
אדון: xviii 6 xxviii 7
אדם: xxii 10 xxiv 15
ואדם: xviii 7
לאדם: xviii 4
אהבתי: xix 12
אהבתיך: xxii 2
אוהבי: xix 6
או: xxii 9
המתאוים: xxii 4
אור: xxvi 11
ואור: xxvii 2
כאור: xxvii 2
ואורה: xxvii 4
אז: xxvi 12
אזי: xxviii 13
האזין: xxviii 8
אוזני: xxi 14
אוזנכה: xxiv 4
אומ[צם]: xxiv 15
מאו[צרותיו]: xxvi 15
אחֵי: xix 17
אחַי: xxviii 3, 9
מאחר: xxviii 11
ואחריו: xxvi 10
אין: xix 9
איש: xxii 10
אוכל: xxvi 13
אוכלמה: xviii 11
אֶל: xxvii 3
אַל: xix 14, 15, 16 xxiv 5, 7, 11
ואל: xviii 2 xxiv 5 *bis*, 10 *bis*, 12, 13
אלה: xxvii 11
אלוה: xxviii 7
אלוהים: xxviii 10, 13
אלַי: xxiv 3, 12
אליך: xxii 7
אליכה: xxiv 3
אל[?: xxi 17
אלפים: xxvii 5, 10
אמונה: xix 14
אמונתכה: xix 9
אמרתי: xxviii 5
נאמרה: xviii 11
אמרה: xviii 13
אמריהמה: xviii 12
אמת: xxvi 10
האמת: xxiv 6
ואמת: xxvi 10
אנוכי: xxviii 14
אני: xix 11, 13 xxi 11 xxii 2 xxviii 5
ואנשים: xxvii 3
באף: xxii 11
מאפלה: xxvi 11
ואצבעותי: xxviii 4
וארבע: xxvii 9
ארבעה: xxvii 6, 10
ואבעים (וארבעים): xxvii 9
ארבעת: xxvii 10
ארץ: xxvi 14
אשר: xxvi 12 xxvii 9, 11
את: xix 8, 11 xxiv 4, 9 xxvi 12 xxviii 6 *bis*, 7, 8, 14
ואת: xxiv 8
אתה: xix 4, 16 xxiv 13

בה: xxi 16 *bis*
בי: xix 15 xxiv 13
בך: xxii 3
בכה: xix 18
בם: xxviii 10
מבדיל: xxvi 11
באה: xxi 11
לבוא: xxii 3
תביאני: xxiv 10
נבחן: xxii 10
בחר: xxviii 10
ונבון: xxvii 3
נבונה: xxvii 4
אתבונן: xxi 17
הבינני: xxiv 8
ובית: xix 17
בן: xxvii 2 xxviii 3
בבני: xxviii 11
ובני: xviii 8 xxiv 15
מבני: xxviii 3
בניך: xxii 7
בנה: xxiv 5
תתבעך: xxii 14
בקר: xviii 8
ובקשתי: xxiv 4
ובקשתיה: xxi 11
בריתו: xxviii 12
אברכך: xxii 12
ברוך: xix 7 xxii 2 xxvi 13

לברכה: xxii 1, 12
וברכות: xxii 13
הברותי: xxi 17
בשר: xix 4
בבשול: xxi 12

גואל: xviii 15
הגבהים: xxviii 9
והגבעות: xxviii 6
גב[ו]רה: xxviii 13
בגדיותיו: xxviii 4
גדול: xxvi 9
גדולה: xxii 2
גדולתו: xviii 5
יגדל: xviii 14
לגדלני: xxviii 9
מגוך: xxii 6
יגילו: xxii 7
גם: xix 11 xxi 12 xxiv 17
גמולי: xxiv 6
גרע: xxi 12

דבר: xxvii 9, 11
ידבר: xxviii 7
דובר: xxii 14
דברי: xxviii 6
דויד: xxvii 2
לדויד: xxviii 3
ל[דוי]ד: xxviii 13
ידורו: xxii 3
דור: xxii 3
ודור: xxii 3 xxvi 9
לדור: xxvi 9
ודורות: xxii 3
דין: xxiv 6
בדעת: xxvi 11
ודעת: xix 14
דרכה: xxi 13
כדרכו: xxii 10
דרכיו: xxvii 3
אדורשנה: xxi 12
כמדשן: xviii 9

הדר: xxvi 9
יהדרו: xxiv 9
הוא: xxviii 8
הואה: xviii 6
והוא: xxviii 8
הודי: xxi 15
ויהי: xxvii 2, 9, 10
הייתי: xix 10 xxviii 3
היתה: xxi 14
ילך: xxvi 10
להלל: xix 8
הללויה: xxviii 3
המון: xxvi 10

הנה: xviii 13
הרים: xxvi 13
ההרים: xxviii 5

זדים: xviii 13
זה: xxii 9 *bis*
זיז: xxii 4
זכורני: xxiv 10
תזכורי: xxii 6
בזוכרי: xix 12
יזכרו: xxiv 11
אזכירך: xxii 1, 12
זכרך: xxii 2
זמותי: xxi 15
זמרתה: xviii 11
אזעקה: xxiv 14
זר[ים]: xviii 16

החבירו: xviii 1
בחבר: xviii 11
החודשים: xxvii 8
חזון: xxii 13
בחטאי: xix 10
חטאת: xxiv 11
כחטאתי: xxiv 7
לחטאתי: xix 13
חי: xix 2 *bis*, 4 xxiv 7 xxvi 13
חכם: xxvii 2
חוכמה: xviii 3
בחוכמתו: xxvi 14
חלמתי: xxiv 17
וחלמות: xxii 14
תחמל: xviii 14
חמס: xxii 6
וחמשים: xxvii 7, 10
חונני: xix 14
בחונכה: xix 17
חסד: xix 8 xxvi 10
חסדו: xviii 14 xix 6
חסדי: xxii 5
חסדכה: xix 1, 3
חסדיכה: xix 9, 13
חסידיו: xix 7
חסידיך: xxii 6
חסידים: xviii 10 xxii 3
חסיתי: xix 12
לחסרי: xviii 5
חקר: xix 9
חריתי: xxi 15
מחרף: xxviii 14

טהר: xxii 6
טהרני: xxiv 12
וטהרני: xix 14
טוב: xxvi 13
בטוב: xxi 15
כטובכה: xix 5

טובים: xviii 14
לטובים: xviii 1
טמאה: xix 15
טרתי: xxi 16
בטרם: xxi 11

יבש: xxiv 12
מיד: xviii 9, 15
ידי: xxi 17 xxviii 4
בידכה: xix 3
יודה: xix 2
תודה: xix 1
יודו: xix 2
להודות: xix 8
וידידיך: xxii 7
ידעו: xxvi 12
ידעתיה: xxi 13
נודעה: xviii 4
לדעתה: xviii 13
להודיע: xviii 2 *bis*, 3, 4, 12
בהודיעכה: xix 2
יהוה: xviii 3, 14, 15 xix 4, 6, 7, 11, 13, 16 xxiv 3, 6, 8, 12, 13, 15, 16, 17 xxvi 9 xxvii 4 xxviii 10
ליהוה: xxviii 5
יום: xxvii 6
היום: xix 17
ויום: xxvii 6
ליום: xxii 4
ולים: xxvii 8
ימי: xxvii 6, 8
יחד: xviii 1
יחדיו: xviii 12
יינקו: xxii 5
יוסיף: xxiv 15
יוסף: xxiv 12
יעקוב: xviii 7
[מיע]קוב: xviii 16
יפי: xxviii 9
ויפי: xxviii 9
היפים: xxviii 10
יצאו: xxviii 9
ויוצא: xxvi 14
ויצר: xix 15
ירשו: xix 16
ישי: xxvii 2 xxviii 3
[ואי]שנה: xxiv 17
ישעו: xviii 2
ישעך: xxii 4
ישועתך: xxii 3
לישועתך: xxii 8

כבוד: xviii 3 xxiv 13 xxviii 5
כבודך: xxii 4, 5
בכבודך: xxii 15
כבודכה: xxiv 9
נכבדים: xxii 13
בכוחו: xxvi 14
כול: xviii 7 xix 2, 3, 4, 17 xxii 11 xxiv 7 xxvi 12 xxvii 9, 11
בכול: xxii 1, 12 xxvii 3
הכול: xxvii 10 xxviii 7, 8
לכול: xviii 3 xxii 12 xxvi 13 xxvii 6 *bis*
ולכול: xxvii 8
מכול: xviii 13
הכין: xxvi 11
מכין: xxvi 14
מכון: xxvi 11
כי: xviii 3, 6 xix 1, 3, 16 xxi 13 xxiv 7 xxvi 12 xxviii 7
כמה: xviii 13 xxii 8
(על) כן: xxiv 14
כנור: xxviii 4
כסאו: xxvi 11
כפי: xxi 17 xxiv 3
הכפורים: xxvii 8
נכרתו: xxii 7, 10
ויכתוב: xxvii 4

לב: xxi 12
לבו: xxvi 12
לבי: xix 13 xxiv 16
לבב: xviii 5
לבבי: xxii 12
להמה: xix 3
לו: xxvii 4, 11 xxviii 6
לוא: xix 1 xxi 16 *bis* xxii 8 xxiv 7 xxvi 12 xxviii 5, 6, 10
ולוא xix 1, 6 xxi 15 xxii 9
נלוו: xxii 7
לי: xxi 11, 14 xxiv 11, 14
לכה: xix 1, 2 *bis*
ולכה: xix 16
למדני: xxiv 8
למלמדי: xxi 14
לקח: xxi 14
קחי: xxii 13
ויקחני: xxviii 10

מאות: xxvii 5, 7, 9
ממבואיה: xviii 6
מבטחי: xxiv 15
תמגרה: xxiv 5
מה: xxiv 15
מהמה: xix 6
מודי: xxii 1
המועדות: xxvii 8
למות: xix 9
מזבח: xviii 9
המזבח: xxvii 5
מוטטי: xix 2
[למט]ר: xxvi 15
מי: xxii 9 *bis* xxviii 7
ומי: xxviii 7 *bis*
למי: xxiv 14

מים: xxvi 10
במישור: xxi 13
מכאוב: xix 15
מכרוני: xix 10
מלאכיו: xxvi 12
מלט: xxii 9
למלמדי: xxi 14
מן: xxviii 3
ממך: xxii 7
ממני: xxiv 5, 6, 10, 11, 13
מנחה: xviii 8
תמנע: xxiv 5
למעון: xxiv 4
כמעט: xxi 13
ממ[ערכות]: xxviii 14
מערמיה: xxi 17
מעשֵׂי: xxviii 7
ובמעשי: xxii 6
מעשַׂי: xxviii 6
מעשיו: xviii 4, 7
כמעשיו: xxii 10
מעשיכה: xxiv 9
מצאתי: xxi 14
המראה: xxviii 9
משמשחו: xxviii 13
וימשחני: xxviii 11
למושחני: xxviii 8
ומושל: xxviii 4, 11
ומשפט: xxvi 11
משפטיכה: xxiv 8

בנבואה: xxvii 11
נביא: xxviii 13
נביאו: xxviii 8
נביאיך: xxii 5
נביאים: xxii 14
נגיד: xxviii 11
יגיד: xxviii 7
יגידו: xxviii 6
להגיד: xix 9
לנגן: xxvii 10
מנגע: xxiv 12
כמגיש: xviii 8
הנדחים: xviii 6
ניחוח: xviii 9
נמתי: xxiv 16
נטה: xxvi 14
הטיתי: xxi 13
הט: xxiv 4
נער: xxi 11
נעורי: xxiv 11
מנעורי: xxi 13
נפש: xix 3
נפשי: xix 8 xxi 16 *bis* xxii 15 xxiv 5
בנפשי: xxviii 5
נפש[ם]: xviii 15
נפשתכמה: xviii 1

נץ: xxi 12
ינצו: xxiv 13
יציל: xviii 15
ותצילני: xix 10
[ומצי]ל: xviii 16
נשיא[ים]: xxvi 15
תשיגי: xxii 13
נשמת: xix 4
אתן: xxi 14
ותן: xxiv 4
ויתן: xxiv 14
וַיתן: xxvii 3
נתתה: xix 4
נתן: xxvii 11
נתנה: xviii 3

סביב: xxii 10 xxvi 10
סופה: xxi 12
סלחה: xix 13
נסמכתי: xix 13
וסופר: xxvii 2
יספר: xxviii 7
תספר: xix 1
ולספר: xviii 3

ועד: xxi 11
עוגב: xxviii 4
יעידו: xxviii 5
בעוה: xix 15
ועוונותי: xix 10
מעווני: xix 14
עוזו: xviii 2, 4, 12
עוזכה: xix 12
ועול: xxii 7
בעולו: xxii 10
עולת: xxvii 5
עולות: xviii 9
עולמים: xxii 13
לעולמים: xxii 2
עזב: xix 6
מעטר: xix 7 xxvi 13
עיני: xviii 14
יעכסו: xxii 5
על: xviii 7, 11, 14 xxiv 14 xxvii 5, 10
ועל: xviii 11, 14 xix 13
ע[ל]יו: xxiv 13
עליך: xxii 8, 14
עלו: xxviii 6
ויעל: xxvi 15
ועלה: xxi 14
מעלה: xxii 12
עליון: xviii 1, 6, 7, 12 xxii 15
העליון: xxvii 11
לעמו: xxviii 11
עמי: xix 17

ועמים: xxiv 9
עמנו: xix 4
ענבים: xxi 12
ויענני: xxiv 16
עני: xviii 15
העצים: xxviii 6
תתעצלו: xviii 2
בעצמי: xix 16
ערבה: xxii 11
מערמים: xxi 17
עושה: xix 7 xxvi 13
עֲשֵׂה: xix 4
עָשָׂה: xxvi 15
עשו: xxviii 4
מעת: xviii 15
בעתו: xxii 1
עתודים: xviii 8

לפאר: xviii 1
מפאר: xviii 7
מפאריו: xviii 14
תתפארי: xxii 6
הפגועים: xxvii 10
פודך: xxii 15
פותאים: xviii 3
לפותאים: xviii 4
ויתפזרו: xxii 11
פלשתי: xxviii 13
ופני: xxi 16
פניו: xxvi 10
לפני: xxiv 5 xxvii 3, 5
מלפני: xxvii 11
לפניו: xxvi 9
לפניכה: xxiv 7
מלפניכה: xxiv 14, 15
פעמים: xxii 12
תפרע: xxiv 5
פרשתי: xxiv 3
ופשעי: xxiv 11
פתח[תי]: xxi 17
מפתחי: xviii 10
מפתחיה: xviii 5

צדיקים: xviii 10 *bis*
יצדק: xxiv 7
צדק: xxii 9, 13
וצדק: xxvi 11
צדקות: xix 7
צדקותיכה: xix 5, 11
וצדקתכה: xix 3
הצואן: xxviii 11
והצואן: xxviii 6
לצונו: xxviii 4
ציון: xxii 1, 2, 9, 11 *bis*, 14
ובצלכה: xix 12
וצעיר: xxviii 3
צריך: xxii 11

תקבלי: xxii 13
קדוש: xxvi 9
וקדוש: xxvi 9
קדושים: xxvi 9
הקודש: xxviii 11
קודשכה: xxiv 4
ומקהל: xviii 10
קוו: xxii 8
קויתי: xix 16
בקול: xix 6
קולה: xviii 10
בקומתם: xxviii 9
ולקורבן: xxvii 7 *bis*
כקטורת: xviii 9
קטן: xxviii 3
אתקלה: xix 14
קנאתי: xxi 15
[מ]קצה: xxvi 15
קראתי: xxiv 3, 16
לקראתו: xxviii 9
בקרבך: xxii 7
כמקריב: xviii 8
קרן: xviii 16
הקשיבה: xxiv 3
בקשות: xxiv 10

ראה: xviii 7
ראו: xxvi 12
הראם: xxvi 12
ראשי: xxvii 7
רבים: xxiv 9 xxvi 10
רבות: xxii 12
והרבה: xxi 14
רגל: xix 2
רגלי: xxi 13
רוב: xviii 4
ברוב: xviii 9 xxii 4
כרוב: xix 5, 11
וכרוב: xix 5, 11
רוח: xix 14 xxvii 4
ורוח: xix 15
רומי: xxii 14
וברומיה: xxi 16
ורחבי: xxii 14
וברחובות: xxii 5
ורחמים: xix 8
רחמיכה: xix 5, 11
רחקה: xviii 13
הרחק: xxiv 11
הרחוקים: xviii 5
רמה: xix 1
וירננו: xxvi 12
ברנה: xix 8
רועה: xxviii 4
רע: xix 16 xxiv 12

הרע: xxiv 6
רעה: xviii 15
ירצה: xviii 8
רשעים: xxiv 6
מרשעים: xviii 13

בשבע: xviii 11
ואשחקה: xxi 15
שטן: xix 15
שיחתם: xviii 12
ואשימה: xxviii 5
וישימני: xxviii 3, 11
וישישו: xxii 4
להשכיל: xviii 5
תשכילם: xix 3
שכרכם: xxii 1
תשמח: xxii 15
ישמחו: xix 17
ישַׂמחו: xxi 12
אשמחה: xix 18
משנאיך: xxii 11
בשערם: xxviii 10

שאגה: xix 8
שאלתי: xxiv 4, 14
לשאול: xix 10
שבחי (vb.): xxii 15
שבחי (n.): xix 16
שבר: xxiv 16
השבתות: xxvii 7
אשוב: xxi 15
לשוב: xxiv 12
השיבותי: xxi 16
ישיב: xxiv 6
השוממים: xix 17
ושופט: xviii 16
שחר: xxvi 11
שיר: xxvii 7, 8
השיר: xxvii 9
ושיר: xxvii 5, 9
תשכח: xxii 9
תשכחני: xxiv 10
אשלה: xxi 17
ושלום: xxii 2
ושלוש: xxvii 6
שלושים: xxvii 8
שלושת: xxvii 5
שלח: xxviii 8

וישלח: xxviii 10
תשלט: xix 15
ישתלם: xxii 10
שלמה: xxiv 14
שמו: xix 6
שמכה: xix 8, 12
שמואל: xxviii 8
שמים: xxvi 14
בשמן: xxviii 11
שמע: xix 5 xxviii 8
נשמע: xviii 10
וישמעו: xxiv 9
[שמע]תי: xxviii 13
השמש: xxvii 2
השנה: xxvii 6
שנים: xxvii 7
תשפטני: xxiv 7
לשורר: xxvii 5
שורשיו: xxiv 13
ושש: xxvii 5
ששה: xxvii 9
וששים: xxvii 6
שתותמה: xviii 11

בתבונתו: xxvi 14
תבל: xxii 12 xxvi 14
תהלים: xxvii 4
לתהלתכה: xix 9
ותוחלת: xxii 3
תוחלתך: xxii 9
תולעה: xix 1
התור: xxviii 9
בתורת: xviii 12
בתורתכה: xxiv 8
תהלת: xxviii 13
התמיד: xxvii 6
תמיך: xxii 8
ותמים: xxvii 3
ולתמימים: xviii 1
תנובות: xxvi 13
תעיתי: xxi 11
ותפארתו: xviii 2, 7
תפארתך: xxii 4, 5
תקותך: xxii 2, 8
יתקף: xix 12
בתֹרה: xxi 11
תשבחתך: xxii 11

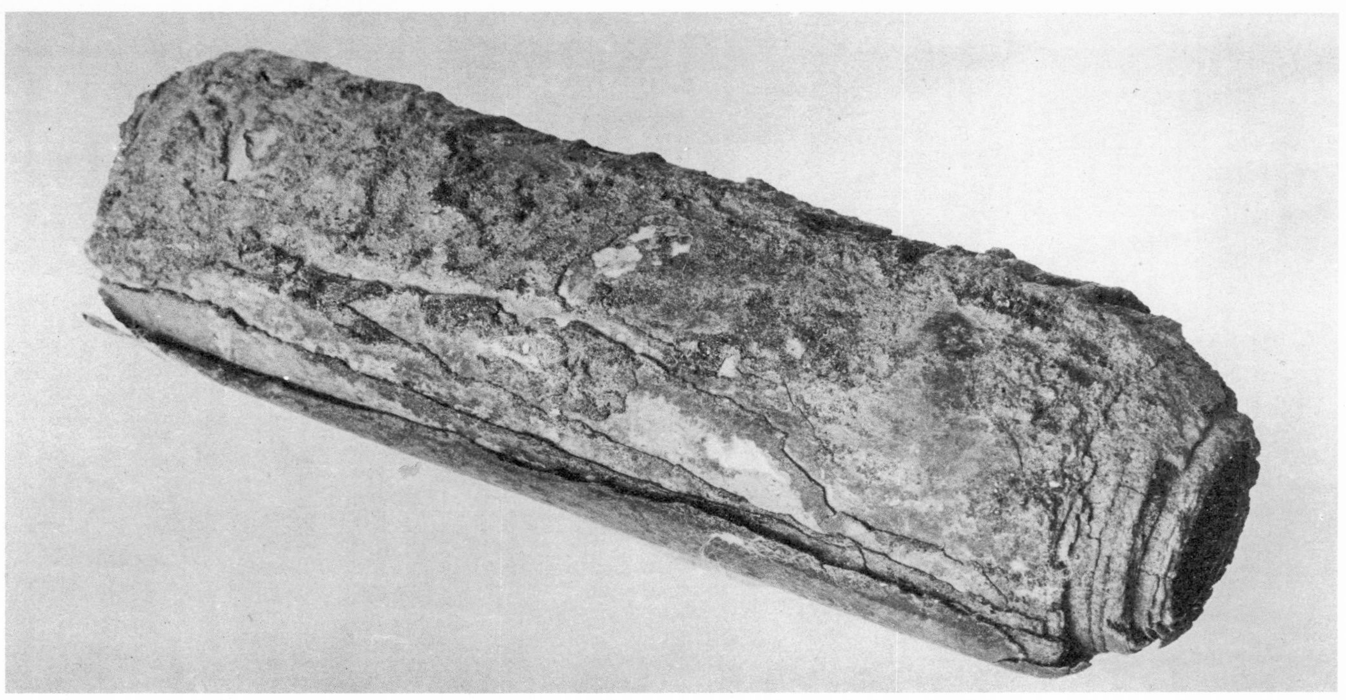

a. The scroll before unrolling, 10 November 1961

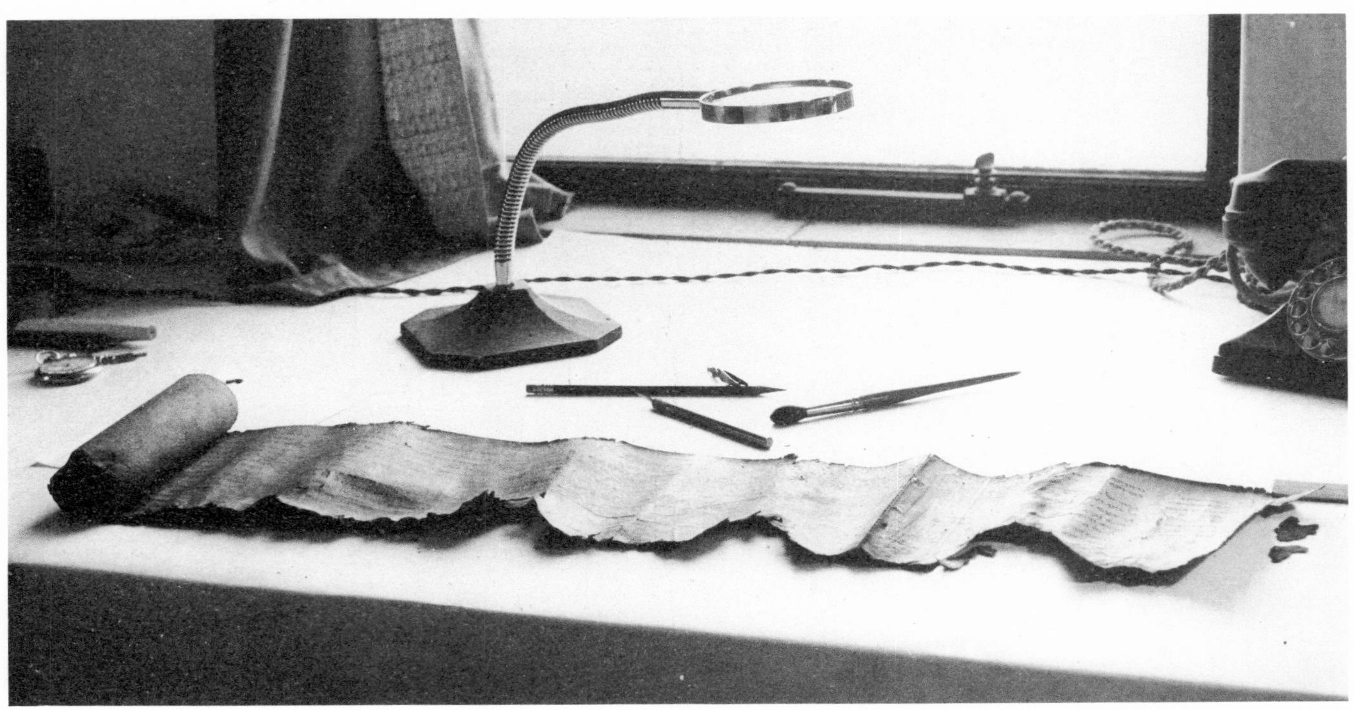

b. The scroll partially unrolled, 16 November 1961

Unrolling completed, 20 November 1961. 11QPs[a] Col. XXIII

Fragments A, B, C I. Pss 101^{1-8} 102^{1-2}

Fragment C II. Pss 102^{18-29} 103 (?$104)^{1}$

Fragment D. Ps 109^{21-31}

Col. I. Ps 105^{25-45}

Col. II. Pss $146^{9-?-10}$ 148^{1-12}

Col. III. Pss 121^{1-8} 122^{1-9} 123^{1-2}

Col. IV. Pss 124^{7-8} 125^{1-5} 126^{1-6} 127^{1}

Col. V. Pss 128^{3-6} 129^{1-8} 130^{1-8}

Col. VI. Pss 132^{8-18} 119^{1-6}

Col. VII. Ps 119^{15-28}

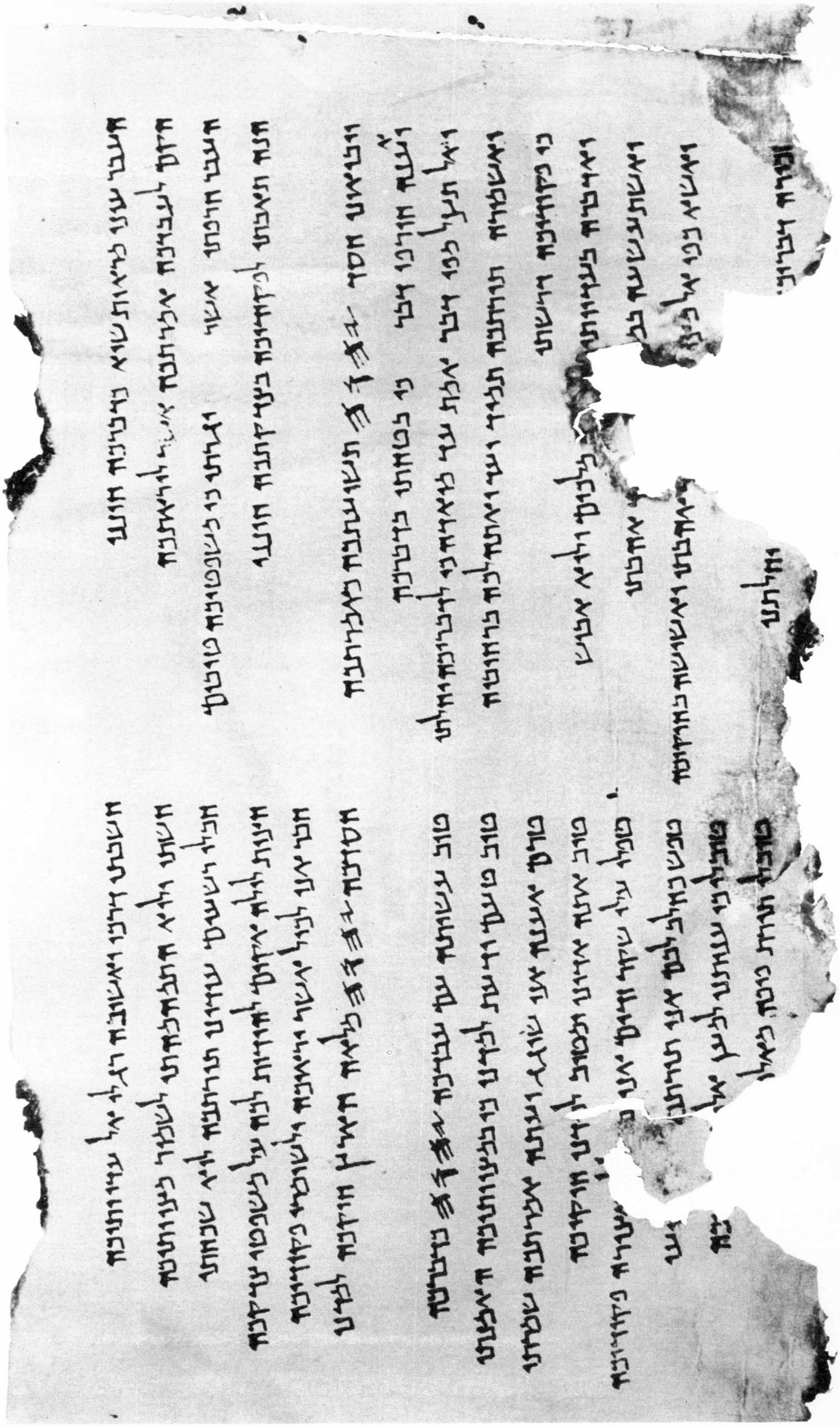

Col. VIII. Ps 119$^{37-49}$

Col. IX. Ps 119$^{59-73}$

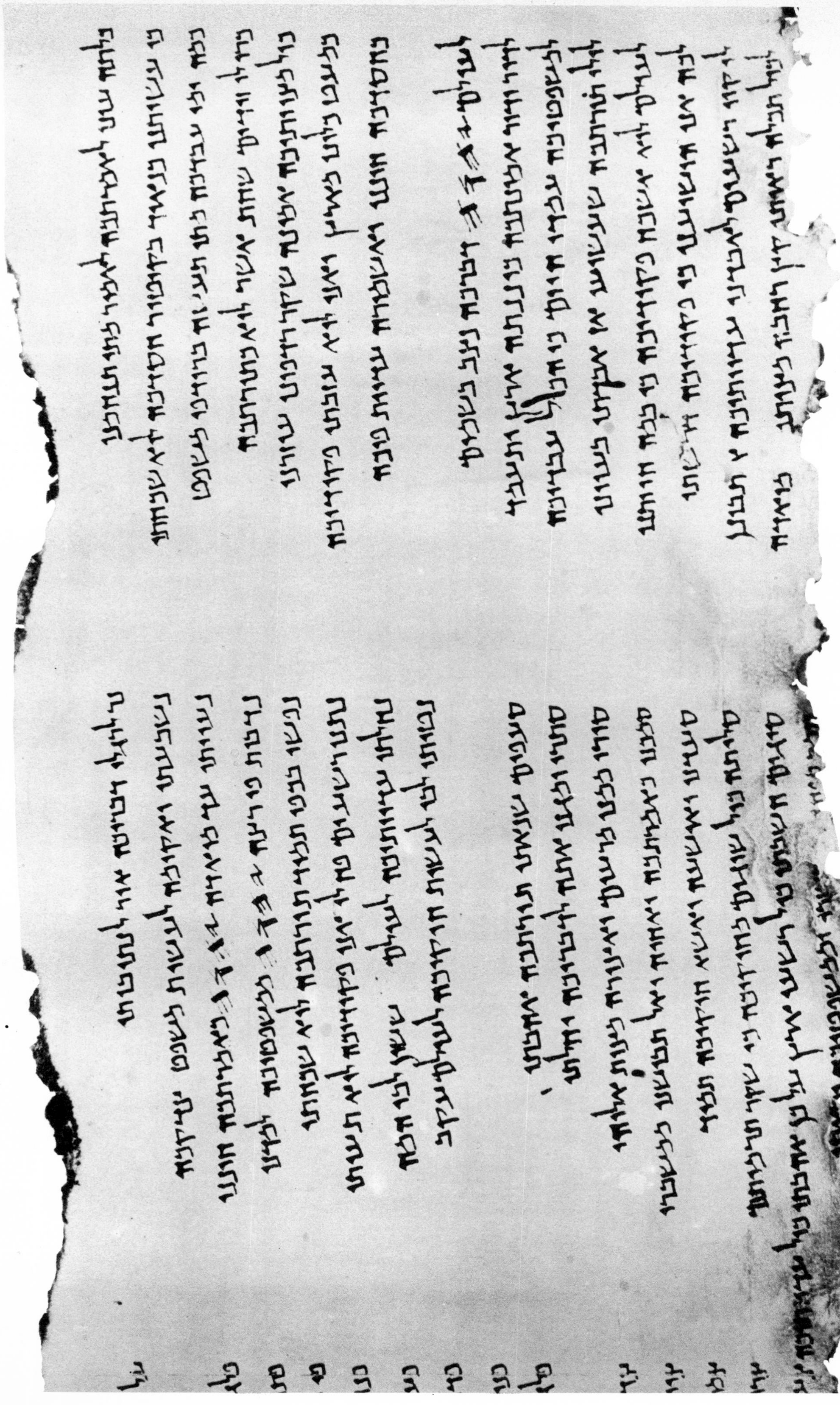

Col. X. Ps 119[82–96]

Col. XI. Ps 119[105–20]

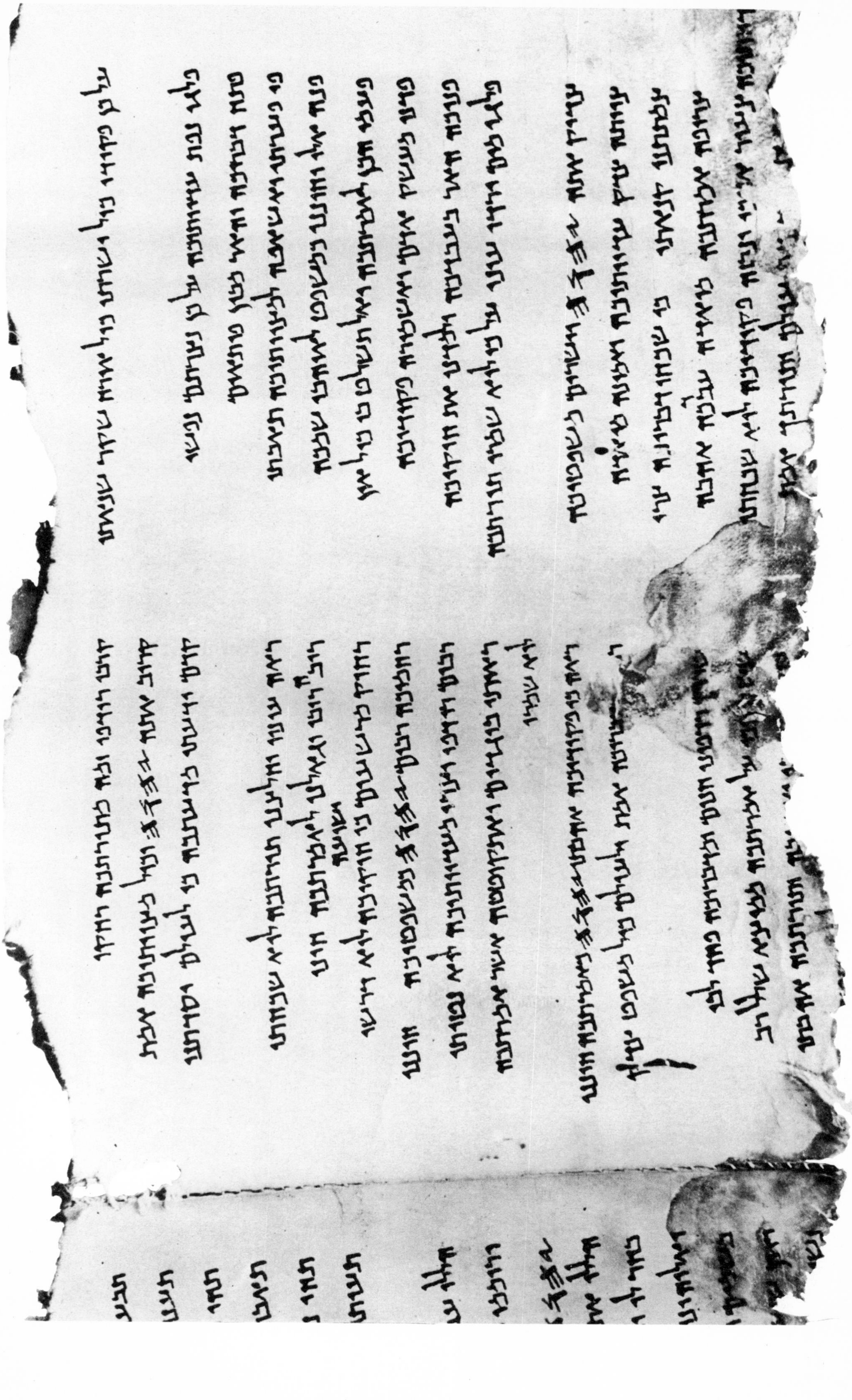

PLATE IX

Col. XII. Ps 119$^{128-42}$

Col. XIII. Ps 119$^{150-64}$

Col. XIV. Pss 119^{171-6} 135^{1-9}

Col. XV. Pss 135^{17-21} 136^{1-16}

Col. XVI. Pss 136^26b 118^1(?), 15, 16, 8, 9, ?, 29 145^1–7

Col. XVII. Ps 145^13–21+?

Col. XVIII. (Syriac) Ps II

Col. XIX. Plea for Deliverance

Col. XX. Pss 139$^{8-24}$ 137^{1}

Col. XXI. Pss 137^{9} 138$^{1-8}$, Sirach 51^{13ff}

Col. XXII. Sirach 51^{30}. Apostrophe to Zion Ps 93^{1-3}

Col. XXIII. Pss 145^{5-10} 133^{1-3} 144^{1-7}

Col. XXIV. Ps 144^{15} (Syriac) Ps III

Col. XXV. Pss 142^{4-8} 143^{1-8}

Col. XXVI. Pss 149^{7-9} 150^{1-6} Hymn to the Creator

Col. XXVII. II Sam 23^{7} David's Compositions Ps 140^{1-5}

Col. XXVIII. Pss 134^{1-3} 151A 151B

DISCOVERIES IN THE JUDAEAN DESERT OF JORDAN · IV

THE PSALMS SCROLL OF QUMRÂN CAVE 11